The Power of Faith

for Teens

True Stories Written by Teens
From the Pages of **Guideposts**.

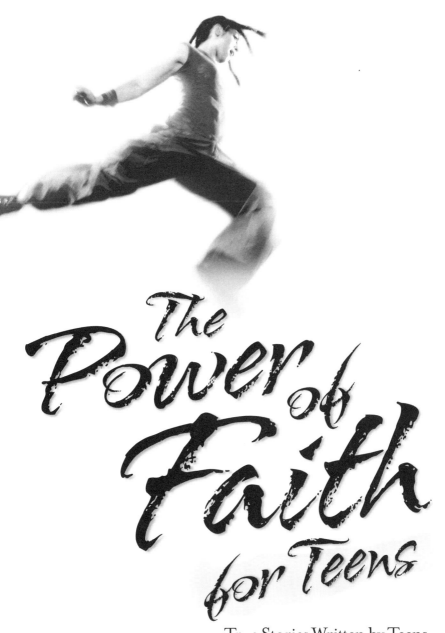

The
Power of
Faith
for Teens

True Stories Written by Teens
From the Pages of **Guideposts**.

Ideals Publications • Nashville, Tennessee

ISBN 0-8249-4622-7

Published by Ideals Publications
A division of Guideposts
535 Metroplex Drive, Suite 250
Nashville, Tennessee 37211
www.idealsbooks.com

Color separations by Precision Color Graphics, Franklin, Wisconsin

Printed and bound in the U.S.A. by RR Donnelley

Library of Congress CIP data on file

ACKNOWLEDGMENTS
CARMICHAEL, AMY. "As Corn Before the Wind" and "A Quiet Mind" from TOWARD
JERUSALEM by Amy Carmichael. Copyright © by The Dohnavur Fellowship. Used by
permission of Christian Literature Crusade, the publisher. GRAHAM, RUTH BELL.
"Dear God, let me soar . . . ," "Lord when my soul is weary . . . ;" "Not fears I need
deliverance from . . .;" from RUTH BELL GRAHAM'S COLLECTED POEMS. Copyright © 1977,
1992, 1997, and 1998 by Ruth Bell Graham. Used by permission of the publisher,
Baker Book House Company.

10 9 8 7 6 5 4 3 2 1

Contents

Now faith
is the substance
of things
hoped for,
the evidence
of things not seen.
-Hebrews 11:1

Preface

The following stories are personal
experiences written by those teens who lived them.
Each tells of a situation in which the teen experienced faith as the
"substance of things hoped for, the evidence of things not seen."

In some of the stories, the writer's faith led him or her to act
without regard to his or her own safety. Other stories show that the
writer has, perhaps unknowingly, been prepared for this moment—
through physical, mental, or emotional training. But in each
instance, it was faith that carried these teens through the task.

Still other stories demonstrate how the writer's secure faith
allowed the author to never give up, to never stop believing that the
circumstance would work out. Plus there are gripping stories of
teens' salvation, both physical and spiritual; and finally, we've
included stories of how faith can demonstrate the love of God.

We hope that this collection of stories will inspire and
encourage teens everywhere. If this book has encouraged you,
please let us know; and send along your own story of how faith
helped you. Send your typed manuscript to: The Power of Faith,
535 Metroplex Drive, Suite 250, Nashville, TN 37211. Include
your name, address, and telephone number. We cannot return
your manuscript; but we will contact you if we publish your story.

What room is there for troubled fear?
I know my Lord, and He is near;
And He will light my candle, so
That I may see the way to go.

There need be no bewilderment
To one who goes where he is sent;
The trackless plain by night and day
Is set with signs, lest he should stray.

My path may cross a waste of sea,
But that need never frighten me;
Or rivers full to very brim,
But they are open ways to Him.

My path may lead through woods at night,
Where neither moon nor any light
Of guiding star or beacon shines;
He will not let me miss my signs.

Lord, grant to me a quiet mind,
That trusting Thee, for Thou art kind,
I may go on without a fear,
For Thou, my Lord, art always near.

AMY CARMICHAEL

Led by Faith

Trapped in a Cavern

Christy Di Frances

I had never been in a cave before, and I was amazed at how cold, damp, and really dark it was. Even though I was with my sister, Annie, and the rest of my church youth group, I couldn't help feeling alone.

"It's freezing in here!" Sarah said.

Peter laughed. "Don't be a wimp! I bet it's at least fifty degrees—almost shorts weather!"

"Hey, Pete, check this out!" Phil called, posing beside a steep precipice. "One wrong step and I fall into the black oblivion!"

"Stop it, Phil," Sarah said. "You're going to scare people."

"Only the freshmen," he said, with a sidelong smirk toward my friend, Christina.

"Okay, knock it off, everybody," our youth pastor, Dave, told us. "Let's have a word of prayer before we start exploring."

As we gathered, my mind drifted back over the past week. We were on our annual youth group summer trip, and we had driven all the way from Wisconsin to spend five days repairing homes for elderly and disabled people in the Appalachian Mountains of Tennessee. We had hoped to go climbing and rappelling today, our last day before returning home, but there had been a massive thunderstorm the night before. We woke up to collapsing tents, soggy clothes, and rivers of mud running through our campsite. Pastor Dave decided that rappelling would be too dangerous in the wet, slippery weather.

We were disappointed until Brad, our project leader in Tennessee, came up with another suggestion. He'd take us exploring in a cave that he had already been to several times that summer. It sounded like fun, so we piled into the vans and headed off.

After Pastor Dave finished his prayer, Brad stepped forward. "Everyone needs to pick a buddy. You'll keep track of your buddy at all times, as we move from cavern to cavern. With the cold temperatures in here, it's dangerous to get lost. You aren't going to last long in a cave like this—especially alone."

"Yeah," Peter said, "and once your flashlight dies, you are a real goner."

Christina grabbed my arm. "Let's be buddies," she said, as we followed Brad across the rocky floor of the cave. He led us through caverns so large that our flashlights could barely pierce the darkness and passages so small that we had to squeeze through sideways. At the entrance of one cavern, he stopped. "Here's something you've got to see."

I rounded the corner and stared. Before us lay a shallow pond as still and smooth as glass, with luminescent stalagmites jutting upwards from the shoreline like miniature mountains. "Wow! Awesome!" I whispered to Christina.

Out of the corner of my eye, I noticed Brad talking with Phil and Peter. He was gesturing toward a narrow passage in the rock. The guys responded with excited nods and followed him.

Christina tugged my arm. "Let's go! Brad's leaving." We scrambled to catch up with the guys as they began a single-file descent through the passageway. Before long, we were crawling on our hands and knees, and within minutes there was only room for us to slide forward on our stomachs. I tried to ignore my uneasiness. Ahead of me, Christina slowed her pace. "Listen," she called back to me. "Do you hear something?"

I stopped for a moment. I did hear a sound. It was water—rushing water. And suddenly there was Brad's voice, calling from the darkness below. "Go back!" he yelled. "Go back! The cavern's flooded!"

I tried to push myself backward, but the passage was too steep and slippery. There was no room to turn around! We were trapped in a tunnel the width of a garbage can. "I can't go back!" I wanted to scream, but my voice was only a scared whisper.

"There's no room to turn around!" someone yelled from behind me. "We have to go down!"

"How many people are back there?" shouted Brad. He sounded worried. " I thought it was just Pete and Phil following me down here!"

As the dozen of us yelled back to Brad, I began to panic. We weren't supposed to follow Brad! Now we were all trapped. We were going to drown miles and miles below the surface! But we had to keep going. The faint beams of our flashlights flickered against the narrow tunnel while sharp rocks scraped our legs. As we crawled deeper, the dank air became colder and the stone passage felt slimy. The sound of rushing water grew louder and louder.

Ahead of me, Christina disappeared. "Christina!" I shouted. No answer. I crawled until the passage became steep, ending in a small cavern—a cavern filled with water. I froze, shining my flashlight down at the murky water and imagining how icy it would feel against my skin. Then I saw Sarah below, holding out her hand. "You'll be all right," she said. There's room for you to turn around. Just slide down feet first." The sight of her standing there so calmly in the deep water gave me courage. I slowly turned around and slid into the cavern.

The water was freezing! It seemed to sap all the strength from my body. Breathe, just breathe. I closed my eyes and tried to force my stiff muscles to relax. Sarah shook my shoulder. "Don't think about the cold," she said. "Listen to me. The others have gone on to the next cavern. It's flooded, too, but it's a lot bigger. We can all fit in there."

I looked around. I didn't see any other cavern, only thick walls of rock all around us. "Where's the entrance?" I asked.

Sarah pointed her flashlight down. "Beneath the water," she said. "Brad found an opening in the rocks. You have to swim through it to get to the next cavern." I looked at her in disbelief. She squeezed my shoulder again. "You can do it. Just a few seconds underwater, then you'll come up beside everyone else."

I nodded, took a deep breath, and ducked beneath the surface. All at once, swirling water was rushing into my eyes and ears, leaving a bitter taste on my lips. Praying frantically, I felt my way through the opening in the stone, and in another moment I surfaced in the next cavern. I blinked away the muddy water and made out several flash-lights along the wall. Everyone was clinging to a rock ledge on the left side of the cavern.

It was like something from a scary movie. But these weren't actors—they were my friends! I spotted Christina, next to Phil and Peter. And Jason, one of the guys in my class. And my sister, Annie! I hadn't known she was down here. I had figured that she was with the rest of the group in the cavern far above us, where it was safe. I stood up—and the water came up to my neck. "Stay to the left!" Jason called out. He jerked his head toward the right wall of the cavern. "The drop-off over there has created a whirlpool."

I gripped the rock ledge with both hands and glanced over my shoulder at the swirling water.

"Is it strong?"

"Not too bad, just keep away from it." He tried to smile, but his eyes were worried. He was pale, too—his skin whiter than I've ever seen it.

We could all freeze to death in this water! I thought. Hand over hand, I pulled myself carefully along the ledge, until I saw Brad speaking to Peter and Brett. "I think I can find a way out of here," he was telling them. "This passageway," he said, pointing toward a hole in the cavern ceiling, "should lead to a wall that we can climb to get back to the main level of the cave.

Brett shook his head. "Should lead to a wall? I don't like the sound of that. Can't we try to go back the way we came?"

"Not a chance," said Brad. "The passageway is way too slippery for most of these kids to crawl back up."

"Brad's right," Peter said, with a wary glance at Jason's pale face and blue lips. "Our best shot is for him to go right now. We've got to get out of here—soon."

I watched silently as the guys gave Brad a boost and he disappeared through the ceiling. The time dragged after he left. No one talked much. The water was so cold—and there wasn't much to say. Finally, Phil spoke up, his voice calm and confident, just like always. "I have the greatest joke for you guys."

I tried to laugh through chattering teeth. "Tell us, Phil."

"So there's this guy who lives on a hill . . ." Phil didn't stop after the first joke; he just kept right on telling them. Soon, our laughter rose above the sound of the rushing whirlpool.

"Thank you, God," I prayed. "Thank you for Phil's sense of humor."

After awhile Peter said, "Brad's been gone forever. Do you think we should follow?"

"I don't know," said Brett, "but we've got to get out of this water. Jason can't stop shaking."

"Brad could have gotten stuck," said Phil. "Someone has to go up after him."

"Someone small," Brett added. Annie was beside him in a moment. "I'll go," she offered.

My heart started pounding. Not my sister! Peter and I looked at one another. "Okay," Peter said. "But if you feel like you might get stuck, turn around. Got it?" Annie nodded. "If you get on my shoulders, you should be able to reach the hole."

We watched Annie vanish into the blackness above. Several minutes later, Brett, standing directly beneath the hole, heard her call down to us. I splashed over to him. "What did she say?"

"She said we can start climbing."

Peter sprang into action. "Brett can climb up first. Phil and I will stay here and lift everyone else up to him."

Brett climbed through the hole in the ceiling and held out his hand to help Christina. Then it was my turn, and Peter lifted me to Brett, who pulled me up onto the ledge where he stood. "Almost there," he grinned, Then he pointed upward. "See that light above us?" A faint glimmer shone through a barrel-sized opening in the rocks high above. "Just climb toward it." I nodded and began making my way up the nearly vertical wall, grabbing whatever hand-holds I could find in the jagged stone. As I climbed, the pale beam of light grew stronger and stronger, and I could hear the hum of voices. Finally, I reached my hand through the opening in the rocks. Strong arms pulled me out of the darkness and into the light.

Someone handed me a dry sweatshirt, and I joined in the hugs and tears as, one by one, those of us who had been trapped emerged from the cave. When the last person surfaced, we bowed our heads and thanked God for his awesome protection. As I closed my eyes, I remembered how I had entered the cave that morning feeling alone. God had shown me that he had been with me—and my friends—all along.

Missy & Mr. Jesus

Missy Alter

s morning dawned, the angry words of six children in a household filled with turmoil could be heard drifting through the windows. It was an argument my mother faced each day as she struggled to hold our family together.

Since she was sick, I am sure Mommy dreaded facing this same confrontation each morning. The task of getting my brother, four sisters, and me off to school was hers alone. My daddy usually spent the nights away on drinking binges. We dreaded his coming home, for he was verbally and physically abusive.

One evening, there came a knock at the door. All six of us children ran to the window; we rarely had company. Mommy answered the door, and Mrs. Jenkins, the social worker, came in, along with a young woman I didn't know.

"Great," Daddy groaned, "another social worker. Ain't nobody comin' here and takin' my young-uns. They're mine by rights and that's final."

"Excuse me," Mrs. Jenkins interrupted. "I'm here to introduce Carol Stallops to your oldest daughter, Carol. For the past three months we have been looking for a Big Sister for her. We've finally found this lovely young lady and I'd like your Carol to meet her."

Daddy didn't say anything as my sister excitedly jumped up and down. She ran over, and Miss Carol gave her the biggest hug my five-year-old eyes ever did see. My sister looked up at Miss Carol and said with a big proud grin, "We got the same first name!"

"Yes," replied Carol, "and we will have a lot of fun together."

That night was the beginning of a change in my life. My sister Carol and I were close; now I was losing her to some strange lady. I envied Carol because I wanted someone for my very own too.

Almost every night, Miss Carol came to take my sister somewhere. Each time Carol left, I cried. I wanted so much to be included in their fun.

One night after she left, I ran out the back door, slamming it behind me, running as fast as my feet would carry me to the woods behind our house. I ached with loneliness both for my sister and for someone of my very own to do things with. I remembered that my Sunday school teacher said we could pray to Jesus when we felt we had no one else to talk to. I did not know how to pray, but I began.

"Mr. Jesus," I began, "you know I ain't got a home like other little girls, and you know Daddy is always drinkin' and beats up on Mommy, and then they come and take her away in that rescue squad truck, and we never see her for a long while. We stay by ourselves and I'm mad 'cause there's no one to care for us. Mr. Jesus, I really want a Big Sister like Carol has so I can get loved all by myself and go places and have fun too. I guess that's all, Mr. Jesus. I hope you heard me. I'm just Missy."

After praying in the woods, I went back to the house. I sensed something was wrong. It was the silence from inside. I tiptoed into the kitchen, and peeked into the living room. I held my breath as I watched Mrs. Jenkins leading my sisters and brother out the front door. As soon as a van carried them all away, a police car arrived and two policemen came up on our porch and pulled my daddy off the old stuffed chair and placed him in the car and drove away. After what seemed to be an eternity, I turned and crept into the bedroom.

"Missy, why aren't you with the rest of the kids?" Mommy asked. I just stood stared. I could see that Daddy had hit her again. Crying, she reached down, picked me up, and hugged me tight.

"Honey, Mommy promises that someday you will have a good home with people to take care of you and give you lots of love."

My brother and sisters were placed in foster homes, but I stayed with my mom. I wished that Mr. Jesus would answer my prayer, for things were getting worse and I was more lonely and scared.

One day my daycare teacher woke me from my nap and told me to go into the playroom. Rubbing my sleepy eyes, I got up and went. There in front of me stood a man and a woman and something told me that Mr. Jesus had answered my prayer.

"Missy," said Mrs. Jenkins, "Mr. and Mrs. Alter want to be your big brother and big sister. They have doggies for you to play with. Would you like that?"

"You bet I would!" That very day Mr. and Mrs. Alter took me to the city park for the most wonderful time in my life.

Mommy became very sick, so I spent all of my time with my new friends, whom I loved and I knew loved me. Mommy was admitted to the hospital in critical condition. Each day she grew worse. She summoned the Alters to her bedside one day and told them she knew that she was going to die soon.

Then she asked, "Will you adopt Missy and take care of my baby?" They grasped her hands and agreed. Soon after that Mommy died. The adoption went smoothly. I was a seven-year-old girl who had everything she ever wanted in life: love and a happy home.

Ten years have passed since the adoption, and I thank Jesus for taking me out of a life of hopelessness and filling me with love and purpose. My prayer for a big sister was answered in a way far greater than I could have imagined. Since the day I became a part of the Alter family, I have known beyond a doubt that there is nothing too great for God to do.

Cast Me Not Off...

Voigt Smith

*I*t had been a week since my eighth birthday, and I was still enjoying all the attention. I was savoring my last few spoonfuls of breakfast grapefruit when my father spoke sternly. "Voigt," he said, "your great-grandma is coming to be with us tomorrow, and I want you on your best behavior."

I dropped my spoon into the bowl. "How long is she going to stay?"

"She's going to live with us, and I want you to help her."

I sat and stared. I was not looking forward to tomorrow.

The next day came, however, and so did Great-grandma. I wasn't the overjoyed person I pretended to be as I kissed her and took her things to her room.

In my mind, three things made our relationship difficult. First, she meant extra work. She couldn't walk, see, or hear very well, so I couldn't keep my play areas as disastrously messy as usual. In addition to having to keep my toys picked up, I was given numerous chores, from making my bed to cleaning the bathroom.

Another thing I didn't like was introducing her to my friends. Like me, they were uncomfortable around people her age, and the introductions were embarrassing. Because Grandma couldn't hear well, her voice was always loud and coarse.

Her physical state was what really bothered me. She seemed so different from most people that she scared me. She grunted at times, she often spent her time just looking out our front window, and she looked as if she were dead when she fell asleep in her chair.

When she had visited in the past, it had taken me a long time to get used to her. Now, she seemed so much older and more pressure was on me to try to be a loving grandson. I was appointed to take tea to Grandma, which really made me feel like a slave. She always thanked me, but somehow this chore was the last straw. I did a pretty good job of holding back my feelings until one day when Mom came into the TV room with a tray. It was filled with Grandma's cup and small cream and sugar containers.

"Voigt," she said, "will you please take this to Grandma?"

I didn't answer.

"Voigt!"

"I don't feel like it!" I snapped. As she opened her mouth to reply, I exploded. With a powerful blow, I knocked the whole tray out of her hands and jumped to my feet in rage. "I hate taking tea to Grandma," I shouted, "and I can't stand living with her!"

I quickly ran to my room. Mother gave me a chance to cool down before she came into the room. She found me sitting on my bed looking through my baseball cards and sniffling. I looked up at her and noticed she was holding a black leather album and a tattered Bible.

"I thought you might like to see some of Grandma's old things." To my surprise, she set them down and left the room. I waited until the door was shut before I opened the album. It contained pictures of everyone from Grandma's grandparents to her great-grandchildren. I was fascinated by the photographs of Grandma as a young woman; she had really been attractive. Finishing the album, I leafed through the Bible, glancing at the passages she had underlined. Like magic, two phrases spoke out to me: "Cast me not off in the time of old age" (Psalm 71:9) and "They shall still bring forth fruit in old age" (Psalm 92:14).

I read them again. Somehow those words from the Psalms broke through the rebellious barriers of my mind. They made sense to me. and they gave me new confidence and patience toward Grandma. I decided to make an effort to show her more love.

Those verses stayed with me; and as the days went by, I became more aware of Grandma's good points. I even asked my friends to say hello to her when they came over. She made me smile when she teased me about my crush on my teacher. I made her laugh by telling her that she was just jealous. She started showing an interest in my car magazines, and I, in turn, showed interest in her stories about our family. Our relationship began to improve. After a while I started calling her "Super Grandma." which almost always brought a smile to her face.

I had always thought of Grandma as old and irritable. Now, however, I began thinking of her as a real person, and it made my extra chores more tolerable. When I took the tea tray to where she sat in our green chair next to the front window, she would tell me about the birds and animals she saw. Grandma kept surprising me. Sometimes I would find her looking through teen magazines. At other times I would find her praying with her hands clenched tightly together. I decided she was young in her heart and old in her ways.

A couple of years later, Grandma left for a brief visit with my uncle. I was surprised to find myself asking when she would be back. I hadn't realized that I would miss her. When the phone rang one day, I was the first to answer, and I recognized Uncle Dave's voice. "Grandma died this morning," he said. His words sent chills up my spine, and my head became dizzy. As I listened to his words of sympathy, I thought of Grandma and the way we had become used to each other. Her death didn't seem possible. Grandma's life had become more a part of mine than I had realized. I had learned to live with Grandma, and now I was going to have to learn to live without her.

Written Proof

Kristen Jobe

C'mon, guys! Let's go!" I yelled to my two girlfriends, jingling my car keys like an alarm bell. "My curfew is midnight." Waving goodbye to everyone else, the three of us raced to my Grand Cherokee. Gossip and giggles filled the Jeep as we roared down the gravel driveway. We'd stayed too late, and I knew my parents would be mad. But it was Saturday night. When you're a teenager, party time is what life's all about, isn't it? Getting into a little trouble at home would be worth it.

"What's that?" Melissa asked, pointing ahead. Smoke smothered the next rise in the road. When we reached the top of the hill, we saw a car smashed into a tree. The engine was in flames. I hit the brakes and threw the Jeep into park. "Wait here," I ordered my friends. My feet hit the pavement, as if I knew what to do. I ran to the demolished car. Smoke engulfed me and I coughed and gagged. I bolted to the passenger side. A man's bloody arm hung from the passenger window.

I screamed, clapping my hand over my mouth. Then, from the car, I heard a shaky voice. "Please," the man called. Panic filled me. "What am I doing?" I asked myself. I looked up through the smoke at the stars high above. "God, I can't do this!" I said.

Then the man called to me again: "Please."

Somehow I had to save him. I grabbed the frame of the door. It was scorching hot, and I jerked my hands away. "Help!" I called. I grabbed the door again. I ignored my pain and pulled with all my strength, but the door wouldn't budge. I cried out once more, "I can't do this by myself!" Then the door frame began to bend. Had someone come to help me? Somehow I seemed to have more strength. I kept pulling.

When the door was bent enough for me to crawl inside the car. "I can't see you," I said, but I felt around till I could grab the man's body. He was unconscious, but still breathing. I inched him toward the door and heaved him out onto the ground. Loud pops burst from the blazing vehicle. I had to get the man to safety. "Give me strength," I prayed as I dragged him as far away as I could. Within moments the car exploded into a fiery ball.

I took my cell phone from my jacket and punched 9-1-1. Still holding the injured man, I sat back to wait for the ambulance. The man stirred in my arms, and I looked closely at him. His face was leathery with age, and he stared at me with hazel eyes. I asked his name. "Harry," he whispered.

"Is there someone you want me to call?" I asked.

Harry motioned to a small book in his shirt pocket, then slipped back into unconsciousness. I took the book from his pocket. A single phone number was written in blue on the inside front cover. I punched in the numbers. A woman answered, and I asked if she knew a man named Harry. "I'm his wife," she said.

My parents were waiting up for me when I got home after dropping my friends off. "Sorry I'm late," I said. I apologized for disobeying them and then told about what happened. "That man's wife was so worried when he didn't come home on time, and it made me think of how you must worry about me when I'm late. I promise never to miss curfew again."

The next morning I went to the hospital and learned that Harry would be all right. His wife hugged me, thanking me for saving his life. But I couldn't take the credit. Something had come over me. Something I didn't understand. Then Harry's wife asked how I knew her telephone number. I explained, and she handed me the small address book I recognized from the night before. She opened the front cover, exactly as I had done. "There's no number written here," she said. "Look."

Finally I put two and two together. Being young is okay, and so is wanting to have fun. But there's more to life than the fun stuff, like how much my parents love me, even when I make a mistake. And how God works through us, although we're not perfect. Even my late Saturday night was used to his good purpose. I saw proof of it in writing.

Lexus

Mickey Kleinhenz

I drove my 1986 Oldsmobile, with its crumpled left fender, into the high school parking lot like it was a stretch limo carrying superstars, not just my soccer buddies and I. Today we felt like superstars. Our team had made it to the regional final four, and our big game was only hours away. Swinging into a parking place, I pumped my fist in the air.

BAM!

"Tell me I didn't just hit somebody's car," I cried. I backed up and leaned out the window. Yep, I'd just put a dent in the rear side panel of a brand-new Lexus.

"Man, you are in a heap of trouble," said Julio.

"Not if he gets out of here fast!" said Robert.

"Go park somewhere else," Tony ordered.

I sat there, frozen, my sweaty palms sticking to the steering wheel. My brain kept replaying a video of me crumpling my Oldsmobile's fender three months earlier. Maybe I should just park in the next row, I thought. Nobody will ever know.

I took a couple of deep breaths. In soccer, I recover from a stupid move by concentrating on making my next move a good one. Denting a Lexus definitely qualifies as a stupid move, I thought. I shook off the temptation to bolt and pulled back into my parking spot.

The guys scooped up their soccer bags and spilled out in a hurry. I got out and set my bag on the trunk, slumping against my car.

"Will your folks will take away your license?" Tony asked.

"That's the least of my worries," I said. "My insurance could be cancelled, and it's going to cost me a big chunk of my college savings to pay for this." My plan was to pay for college with scholarships and savings from my part-time jobs. I didn't have enough for the first year yet, and a Lexus repair bill was going to set me back even further.

I stared at the dent. Anybody who can afford to drive a Lexus can afford to repair one, and the damage didn't look that bad. Maybe the driver won't notice it. Maybe I can just ignore it.

Tony grabbed my soccer bag. "Come on, Mickey. I'm tellin' you, leave now and you won't get stuck with any bills."

I nodded my head toward the locker room. "You guys go on. I'm going to wait here. If someone doesn't come soon, I'll leave a note on the car." Julio rolled his eyes. Robert slapped his forehead like I was crazy.

Just then, I saw a girl digging in her purse at the other end of the Lexus. The car must be hers. My buddies scooted toward the locker room as I introduced myself and reported the bad news.

"My name's Rachel," she said. "I really appreciate your admitting to this."

We exchanged information, and I told her I'd pay for the repairs. She agreed to let me work it out without getting the insurance companies involved. I headed for the locker room feeling torn; I knew that I'd done the right thing, but I still felt like the biggest idiot in the universe.

That evening, the soccer competition was so intense that I forgot about the accident. Even though we lost 1–0, Coach said we played the best game of the season. We had faced the top team in the region, he said, and we should hold our heads high.

As I made my way back to the locker room, I looked back at the field. That big fat zero on the scoreboard reminded me of how my bank account would soon look. It was time to go home and tell my parents about the Lexus.

"You were parking the car and did what?" Dad's said.

Mom turned her "you've disappointed us" face toward me and said, "If we claim another accident on your insurance, a lot of agencies are going to refuse to cover you in the future. And in Texas, you can't drive without insurance."

Great, I thought. What else can go wrong?

"You'll have to handle this yourself," Dad said. "It's a good thing the Lexus owner didn't report this to the insurance company right away."

Mom and Dad didn't take away my license. I guess they figured that having to pay for repairs on top of college expenses was plenty of punishment.

When I got home from school the following afternoon, Mom surprised me with a hug. "What's that for?" I said.

"I called the Lexus lady to apologize for the damage you did to her daughter's car," she said. "Her daughter heard your friends encouraging you to leave as she was walking to her car that afternoon. And she heard you refuse."

I nodded.

"The lady praised the mature way you handled the situation. She told me she was sure you would gain your reward in the future."

"Maybe I'll win the lottery, that would definitely cover the repairs to the Lexus."

Mom patted my shoulder. "You did the right thing."

I had to smile. It felt good to be complimented, even if my pockets were empty. I guess I'd made the right move that afternoon in the parking lot, after all.

About a week later, Rachel called with an estimate for the Lexus: $861! Fortunately, she agreed to get another estimate, but she didn't have time to get one for a couple of weeks. I waited and worried. Am I going to be flipping burgers instead of going to college next year?

Senior prom came up during the two weeks of waiting. I would have skipped it because of my money situation, but I had already made plans to go. Thankfully, the senior class had raised a lot of money over the years, so that made the ticket price cheap. I borrowed my brother's tuxedo and managed to spend very little.

After the prom ended, the PTA put on a great party for the rest of the night. They decorated the cafeteria and set up game booths where we could win prizes. The organizers also held prize drawings every twenty minutes. They gave away merchandise, gift certificates, coupons, and cash. I kept praying I'd win some cash, but my name wasn't called. We've been here all night, I thought. I can't believe I haven't won something.

They had saved one big prize for the very end. As I sat at a table with my friend, Johnny, a voice blared over the loudspeakers. "It's time to announce the grand prize winner of your Safe-Prom party!" Everyone cheered.

Johnny elbowed me. "I'll bet a dollar you win the grand prize."

I looked around at the two hundred or more of my classmates who were there. "No way! I'll bet you win the grand prize."

"The winner is Mickey Kleinhenz!"

Johnny pounded me on the back and pushed me to my feet. I wasn't sure if I had really heard my name or not. After all, I'd been up all night and things were kind of fuzzy. But my other friends were smiling and clapping, too. So I went up and accepted the grand prize—a check for two thousand dollars. As I looked down at it, I remembered what the Lexus lady told Mom: You'll gain your reward in the future.

Within a week, Rachel called to say that the latest Lexus repair estimate was only $405. 1 wrote her a check for it and put the rest of my grand prize money in my college fund. All, that is, except for the dollar I owed Johnny.

Drummer Boy

Luke Hollingsworth

H ey, drummer boy," said the flight attendant. "Quit banging on the lap table."

I stopped my tapping and looked up, shooting her an innocent grin. "Sorry!"

It was nearly midnight, and I was tired and edgy. Because of airport delays, my friends and I had been traveling for twenty-four hours already, on our way home to Arkansas from a two-week tour of Germany and Austria. Our college choir had entertained Kosovo refugees there and they had made us feel like we were world-famous entertainers. It had been an awesome trip, so I was sorry to see it end. Before long, summer would be over and it would be time to face all the things I had to do back at school—exams, classes, cheerleading practice—plus look for a job after graduation. Sometimes the pressures seemed overwhelming

I closed my eyes, leaned back, and tried to relax. "We're ninety miles out of Little Rock, starting our descent," announced the pilot. "And there's some bad weather out there, folks. Outside to the left, you can see an incredible light show."

I leaned forward to look out the window, but, the only thing I could see was the top of the wing. Through the flashes of lightning,

I watched huge raindrops riddle the plane like bullets.

Thunder clapped, and the plane shook and rattled as we flew through the storm. I looked around, searching for the familiar faces of my twenty-five classmates, who were sitting throughout the plane. I caught the eye of our choir director a few rows ahead of me. I sat back with a sigh. "We're almost home," I thought. "This turbulence will be over soon."

At last, we approached the airport and heard the wheels drop. Rain and sleet pelted the windows as we descended. We hit the runway hard.

"Thank God!" said a man in my row. "We landed safely."

"Wait!" I thought. I had flown enough times to know that upon touchdown, you should hear and feel the reverse thrusters slowing down the plane. "Something's wrong! We're still at top speed!" As we continued to barrel down the runway, my heart pounded. "We're going to crash!" The plane began to skid, then veered to the right. "We're running out of runway!"

"Brace!" screamed a flight attendant.

I crouched down, grabbed my knees, and buried my face in my lap. A moment later, the plane slid off the runway surface, and we began to spin around, banging and pounding wildly as we tore across grass. I held tight as I jerked around, my seat belt the only thing holding me down.

Finally, we skidded down a slope and slammed hard into something. There was a loud screech, followed by the sound of grinding metal against metal. It sounded—and felt—like the whole plane was being ripped apart.

At last, we stopped. Everything was quiet, except for the torrential rain beating down outside. An eerie stillness filled the dark, cold cabin.

"It's over," I said to the lady next to me.

As my eyes adjusted to the darkness, I realized it wasn't over. The plane was badly damaged—it was too dark to see much up ahead, but I could tell that the tail section of the plane, where we were sitting, had been torn away from the front section. All around me, rows of seats had been ripped out and tossed around. My row had slid into the small area at the back of the plane where they keep the beverage carts.

"Get me out of here!" cried a woman nearby who was trapped under her seat. Other people screamed. "We can't get out!" a man shouted as he tugged at the exit door in the rear of the plane. Several passengers began to throw themselves against the door, trying to force it open.

"Everyone's starting to panic," I thought. "God, what can I do?"

"Calm down!" I yelled. "People need help!"

The people slamming themselves against the door stopped when they heard my voice.

"Okay, let's help these people who are stuck," I said. Several of us began to free passengers who were pinned under seats.

After a few minutes, though, people started banging on the exit door again. "If we can't go this way, let's make our own exit," someone yelled. Passengers pounded on the side of the plane and tore at windows, attempting to escape. But nothing worked. "We're trapped!" I thought. I was starting to get panicky myself.

A moment later, there was a flash. Then smoke poured in, a thick, black fog that rolled from front to back in a smothering blanket. It hit me at chest level, and I dropped instinctively to my knees.

"Get on the floor!" I shouted as I pulled my shirt over my face. I smelled burning jet fuel. I wondered if I was going to be burned alive. I crouched on the floor, unable to help the people who were crying and choking close by.

As quickly as the smoke had rolled in, something sucked it back out. I took a deep breath; some of the panic had left the cabin. Everyone rose to their feet and headed toward the exit door in the back of the plane. But this time, no one shoved.

After a few attempts, we finally inched the door open. A woman in front peered through. "It's a dead end!" she yelled. On the other side of the door, a huge section of the plane's tail had been crushed, preventing our escape. There was no way to move it.

"We're trapped!" screamed the woman. "Turn around!"

A man toward the front yelled, "There's too much fire and smoke. We can't go that way."

"Dear God," I prayed, "there has to be a way out. Please help us find it. Please help me stay calm." Black smoke was seeping in again and everyone was frightened. In the darkness, I strained to examine the walls of the plane. "Look! There's a gap in this seam."

A few of us began to tear at the seam in the wall with our bare hands. The metal panels behind had been bent and twisted in the crash, so we were able to pry through to the outside. Soon, we had ripped a hole big enough for me to squeeze through.

Outside, the storm was raging. Hail pelted me as I stood on a narrow ledge near the opening I'd just crawled through. The ground was pretty far below, but I figured we could jump. It was our only chance. I pulled back the seam to make the opening larger and helped people out. When I was sure everyone had exited, I leaped to the muddy ground below.

I was standing in a field of mud near a small creek, only a few feet from the raging Arkansas River. Thunder roared; and with each flash of lightning, I saw more of the accident scene. The plane had crashed into a tall steel tower and broken into three sections. Flames leaped around the wreckage and I could smell fuel burning. "This whole thing could explode any second," I thought. Everywhere, people were crying for help. Some rolled in the mud, crying and screaming. I realized, horrified, that they were all burned. "Where are the ambulances and fire trucks?" I wondered.

Two girls from my choir saw me and ran over. "Luke, what do we do now?"

"We've got to get everyone across that creek," I shouted. "The plane could explode." The girls and I gathered the people around us and turned away from the plane. Hail, rain, and wind lashed our faces as we started toward the creek.

A few feet away, a lady lay on the ground. "I think something's broken," she gasped as I approached her. "I can't breathe."

Behind us, the flames grew higher, fed by jet fuel. "I'm going to have to carry you," I said and gathered her up in my arms. When we got to the creek, I lifted her onto my shoulders and waded across the chest-deep water.

"God, give me strength," I prayed. As a college cheerleader, I was used to lifting people, but crossing that creek took everything I had.

We waded through the freezing torrent, lightning zapping around us from every direction. "I'm sorry, ma'am," I said as she cried out from the pain. "I'll stop for a second, but we have to get away from the fire."

Finally, I reached the spot on the hill where the others had gathered. I set the woman down in the grass.

"Are you okay?" I was afraid she'd pass out or go into shock.

"I'm cold," she replied.

I took off my shirt from Germany and covered her with it.

"Go help someone else." she said faintly. "I'll be okay."

Further up the hill, I saw my friend, Barrett, guiding injured passengers. He ran toward me, whooping, "Luke! Luke! Praise God, we're alive!" In a bear hug he tackled me to the ground. Good old Barrett. I was never so glad to see him.

"Barrett, we made it!" I said. For the first time, I started to feel relieved, like our nightmare might just be over.

A huge clap of thunder shook the ground, and people near us screamed. Barrett and I looked at each other and realized it wasn't over. There had to be more than a hundred people on that plane, and there were no rescue workers in sight. God had gotten us this far, now we had to go back and help the others.

"Come on," I said, "Let's go back."

We headed for the front section of the aircraft. Barrett knelt to assist an injured passenger, and I went forward. The nose of the plane was crushed. When the lightning flashed, I could see that some metal beams had sliced into the left side of the flight deck and killed the pilot.

In the shadows, I could hear breathing. The copilot was still in his seat.

"Are you okay?" I asked.

"Yes," he groaned.

"I'm sorry, sir, but your pilot is dead."

"Yes," he said. "I think my legs are broken. I can't get out."

Flames crept closer to the copilot. I tried to move him, but he was pinned tight. Dear God, what now? Please help us.

"Listen," I said. "I hear sirens, and they're coming closer. I'll get help." I jumped to the ground and was relieved to see rescue workers racing to the scene.

"Over here," I shouted. "The copilot needs help."

I continued to direct rescue workers to the injured. One woman, a flight attendant, was writhing on the ground in pain as a man tried to stop the bleeding from a huge gash on her forehead. I walked over to see if I could help. When she saw me, she smiled through her tears.

"Why, it's drummer boy."

It was the same flight attendant who had been scolding me for banging on my lap table. "Yes, it's me," I responded.

I held her hand as the man kept pressure on her wound. Only half an hour ago I was nervously tapping on that table, worried about all the pressures that I faced back home. Somehow, those worries didn't seem very big now. God had helped me and all these other people through the fiery horror of this crash. I knew he would be there to help me face whatever problems and decisions lay ahead.

34

A Touch on the Shoulder

Haven Webster

Two winters ago my stepsister, Dana, came to live with us. She was my age, fifteen. Her dad is my stepdad, and he lives with Mom and me and my younger sister, Heidi, in a small town just south of Greensboro, North Carolina. Dana and her brother had lived with their mom in a nearby town. My stepsiblings had spent weekends with us for years, and I had always enjoyed having an extra brother and sister around to play with.

But when Dana hit adolescence, things changed. She changed. One night Dana's mother called and talked to my stepdad for an hour.

"Dana's having some problems," he said quietly. "And her mom wants to get her away from the crowd she's running with." My stepdad paused. "Can we pull together for Dana and have her come live with us for awhile?"

Mom was eager. "Sure we can."

"Of course," said Heidi.

I got this knot in my stomach. The decision clearly affected my life most. She'd have to transfer to my school, my grade. I played on the girls' basketball team; my friends were not a wild bunch. Some were athletes, all of them studied hard, a lot of them went to church.

We respected our parents and followed the rules. That wasn't Dana's way. "Why should her problems now be dumped on us?" I wondered.

"Where's she going to sleep?" I asked, hoping to nix the idea. The three bedrooms in our home were already occupied. "She can't live on the couch, can she?" Mom and my stepdad looked disappointed.

"My bedroom's the biggest," said Heidi. "She can share it with me." And so it was settled.

That winter was the most unpleasant season in the history of our home. Dana brushed in angrily that first night and hardly spoke while Mom and Heidi fell all over themselves helping her unpack and making her feel welcome. I hung back, watching and wondering when the big storm would come. I didn't have to wait long. My stepdad poked his head in the bedroom door. "Let's all go for ice cream!"

"Count me out," Dana said. She made it clear that she wasn't interested in any of our goody-two-shoes activities. My stepdad made her come anyway. We all climbed into the car, none of us with an appetite for ice cream.

Later, alone in my bedroom, I went down on my knees. "Dear Lord, help us get through this. Change Dana so we can go back to normal." But my resentment grew when I heard Mom's footsteps hurrying down toward Heidi and Dana's room to wish them a good night.

Several mornings later I noticed dark circles around Mom's eyes. Because of all the chaos, she wasn't getting enough rest. "This is so unfair," I complained to her.

"Things will get better," Mom said patiently. "Dana needs us." Mom took every opportunity to give her a compliment or a hug. And I wondered, How can Mom try so hard when Dana isn't trying at all?

Dinner at our house became a tense scene. Everyone seemed to be on edge. Gone were the animated conversations. Heidi was her chatty self, but I was definitely quieter. Mom and my stepdad had enough to worry about without listening to my frivolous teenage concerns, like the new outfit I coveted or how hard practice had been.

One night after doing the dishes my stepdad and I went outside to shoot some baskets. While I had him alone, I thought I'd fill him in on what had been going on in my life since Dana's arrival. These days his focus always seemed to be on her. "I walk her to every class; I've introduced her to my friends; I've invited her to basketball games and to just hang out. I've helped her with homework and explained school projects. What else am I supposed to do? What more does she want?"

My stepdad sighed. "I don't know, Haven," he said. "I just don't know." He bounced the ball. I wished I'd kept my mouth shut. Maybe my life wasn't affected most, after all.

For the first time I considered how Dana might be feeling. She'd moved into a new home, and switched midyear to a new school. It couldn't have been easy. I'd gone through the motions with her, but personally I'd pretty much kept my distance. Maybe that wasn't right. "God," I asked at bedtime, "help me to be more sisterly toward Dana."

My nightly prayers became more sincere, but the days always brought more nightmares. Why wouldn't God simply work a miracle and change Dana instantly? She'd been living with us for four long months, and I saw no end to the "temporary" setup.

Then something strange happened. On a night early in April I awakened from a sound sleep. I never wake up in the middle of the night. Normally, a radio playing full blast couldn't wake me, but that night, at 1:00 A.M., something did. At the foot of my bed was an angel. He was clothed in pure white, with a bright light shining all around him. I couldn't see his face—it was surrounded by a sparkle—but when he spoke, his voice was deep, and urgent.

"Tell her before it's too late," he said.

"Tell who what?" I asked.

Reaching toward me, he said, "Tell her before it's too late."

I wasn't afraid, just completely puzzled. "Who?" I asked, mentally going down the list of my best friends' names. Who needed to hear something from me?

The deep-voiced angel simply repeated, "Tell her before it's too late." Then he was gone, and my thoughts that night were full of questions. Why me?

I kept the angel's visit to myself; no one would believe me anyway. I wasn't even sure exactly what had happened—until two nights later.

This time even before I fell asleep, the angel came back. He appeared right beside my headboard and tapped my shoulder to get my attention. His message was the same, but even more urgent.

"Tell her."

"Who?"

"Dana."

And he was gone.

In algebra the next day, I stared at the x's in the equations on the blackboard. What could I tell Dana? That I had been praying for God to change her radically and he was taking his time about it? Looking back, I had to admit she had made small efforts. She cheered at my basketball games, but I figured family was supposed to do that. She had pulled up her grades, though it was either that or be grounded. She was making friends of her own, including some pretty good kids, like Krystal, one of the cheerleaders. And at least she'd stopped bellyaching about going to church. Dana had even joined the choir, which Mom directed. Very un-Danalike.

Now that I thought about it, things were much more pleasant at home. Dana had begun to change. I was the one who hadn't. I was as impatient as ever with God, and I suppose I was somewhat unwilling to share my parents' attention.

Maybe I needed to change some things about myself too.

That afternoon after school I did what I always did when I had a problem: I went to Mom. I told her about the angel's visits. "I know God loves me," I said. "And I love Dana. But I still don't know what to tell her."

"Tell her how you feel," Mom said simply. "Tell her about God's love. Here's your chance to help your sister."

That evening, I got my courage up. "Dana," I said, "there's something I've got to tell you. Will you come on back to my room?" Dana looked at me skeptically. In all the time she'd lived with us, I don't think I'd ever invited her into my private sanctuary.

We sat on my bed. I was tense, not knowing how or where to begin. So I looked her straight in the eye and told her everything, about seeing an angel, about being sisters, and about God's love and how powerful it is. How we can do anything when we know it is for real.

"The angel came because God cares about us," I told her. "He loves us." I began to cry and Dana reached out and hugged me. "I really care what happens to you," I told her.

"I care about you too," she said.

I'd prayed for the change in Dana. But more important, God had changed me. I had asked him to touch one heart, and he took the opportunity to touch two.

Not fears
I need deliverance from
today—
but nothingness;
inertia,
skies gray
and windless;
no sun,
no rain,
no stab of joy
or pain,
no strong regret,
no reaching after,
no tears,
no laughter,
no black despair,
no bliss.
Deliver me
today
. . . from this.

RUTH BELL GRAHAM

Prepared by Faith

From Out of Nowhere

Derek Daniel Pierce

I guess I've given my mom her share of gray hairs in my nineteen years. Once, I was nearly struck by lightning during a freak electrical storm. Another time, I fell out of a second-story window. I've been kicked by a horse, lost at sea for a day and a half, suffered a concussion, and walked away from a wreck that totaled my best friend's car.

Mom likes to say, "Derek, your angel works overtime." I used to think that was just one of her expressions until one night last August when I found myself face-to-face with danger such as I had never known before.

My church group was camping at a large retreat called Glorieta, which is tucked away amid the aspens and high pines of northern New Mexico, about a thousand miles from home in Spring, Texas. I'd graduated from high school that spring and would be starting college in a week. After six years of going to a church youth summer camp, I had finally come far enough in life to attend Glorieta with the college group for student week. In the past, Mom had been one of the staff counselors, but this year I was on my own. I don't mind telling you that, although I love my mom, I was happy about that.

Camp Glorieta is a special place. College kids from around the country gather there every August. It is an incredible experience meeting so many people your own age, especially girls. The leaders are cool, and the directors are great. There are Bible studies and discussion groups, of course, but everything is low-key. It's as if you are on the threshold of adult life and free to make your own decisions about your time. Mostly, Glorieta is a chance to get to know yourself a little better in surroundings that are as beautiful as any I know.

The first night, our group played games and went to a concert. The next morning at Bible study I met a girl named Kendra Brooks from El Paso. She had pretty blond hair that fell around her shoulders and blue eyes, but it was her smile that really got to me. I worked up my courage and invited her to join my study group. We hit it off, and later, we hiked and ate together and talked as if we had known each other forever.

One night we walked to the Prayer Gardens for some quiet time. Kendra's hair seemed to soak up the moonlight and the sky was a silvery spray of stars, a sky you see only in the mountains. I had been skiing in the Rockies but I had never seen them during summer.

When other people showed up, we scouted for privacy. We found a peaceful place about thirty yards behind my cabin. I grabbed a blanket from the cabin for warmth against the night air. We talked about our lives back home. Kendra had recently broken off a relationship and so had I, so we talked through our feelings.

Then we were quiet and listened to the lonely yip of a faraway coyote in the motionless dark. All of a sudden something horrible clamped down on my skull. There was no sound—no warning—just the wet crush of jaws on my scalp from out of nowhere. For a fleeting instant, I thought the guys in my group were playing a joke; but the explosion of pain in my head told me this was real.

I was dragged, then lifted off the ground. Kendra's scream pierced the air and I fell with a thud. Scrambling, I wiped something hot and sticky from my eyes and saw a huge, snarling black bear towering over me.

I grabbed Kendra. I pushed her head into my chest and rolled us into a ball in the blanket. "Play dead," I whispered. We lay perfectly still, trying not even to breathe. Only the pounding of our hearts filled the silence. The seconds seemed to freeze. I prayed as never before, "God, protect us."

Suddenly the bear pawed my back trying to see if I was really dead. I heard a snort and a low growl and sounded as if he were moving away. He's given up, I thought with a surge of relief. Just then the bear charged, lunged with his mouth, and shook the blanket and ripped the shirt off my back. The bear dragged us, tangled in the blanket, another six feet or so until Kendra shrieked again. Startled once more, the animal let go.

Somehow we managed to curl up again in a protective ball, but this time Kendra's back was exposed. The bear hovered and then pounced; he shredded her clothes with his razor claws and slashed her bare skin. Again Kendra let out a high, terrified scream.

Hearing my friend scream like that, I grew angry. I had to do something. Another prayer for protection flooded through me as my adrenaline began to flow. I jumped up and flailed at our attacker, yelling and kicking. Distracted, he turned from Kendra with a nasty snarl. "Run, Kendra," I commanded. "Now." Out of the corner of my eye I saw her stagger to her feet and run. In front of me the bear advanced menacingly.

He must have weighed three hundred pounds. I could feel his footsteps thudding on the ground. He reared up, all six feet of him. We were eye to eye but I was not going to let this bear past me. I needed to give Kendra time to get away. "God, I know you will send help to protect me," I prayed.

I stamped my feet. The bear paused. His breath came in hot puffs of steam, his eyes fiery and fierce. The air was thick with my fear. Yet I stood my ground, not giving an inch. I remembered my mother's words about my angel. I felt the strength of ten men. Then I started screaming and yelling at the beast, waving my arms like a madman, kicking the ground. The bear looked as if he would charge again when suddenly, inexplicably, he backed off. The aggression seemed to drain out of him completely. He lumbered over to some rocks about fifteen feet away and stopped and glared at me.

"Derek," I heard Kendra wail somewhere to my left. It was time for me to run. I tore into the darkness, glancing over my bloody shoulder to see the bear still standing by the rocks, as if frozen. I caught up with Kendra. She grabbed my hand and cried with relief. We ran to my cabin and burst through the door, still wild with terror. A few friends from my group put us in a van and drove like crazy to the camp nurse station. Kendra wept uncontrollably. I tried to comfort her; but as the reality of events caught up with me, I lost it too, and by the time we got to the infirmary she was taking care of me.

I started going into shock and hyperventilating. The nurse administered oxygen to slow my breathing, then cleaned Kendra's badly scratched back and my scalp lacerations. We were lucky we didn't need stitches, but in the morning the camp directors took us to the hospital in Santa Fe, where we were examined thoroughly and began a series of rabies shots.

No bear was going to ruin my Glorieta experience. I stayed the week and when I left for home, Kendra signed a picture for me. "I'll never forget this week or how you saved my life," she wrote. I'll never forget her either. Am I glad she could scream so loud!

I know God sent me help that night. Something made that bear turn away, maybe an angel who screamed even louder and higher than Kendra, so loud that only the bear could hear. What I do know is that now when my mom says, "Derek, your angel works overtime," I no longer write it off as just another one of her expressions. And I make a special effort these days to do what I can not to give Mom any more gray hairs.

Redhounds Football

Travis Freeman

The spirit of Redhounds football runs through Corbin, Kentucky, like tap water. I'd been to their games since before I could remember—falling asleep on my parents' lap, holding a Redhounds pennant. By the time I could walk, I was punting a football over the coffee table. By first grade the guys and I were picking teams in our yards. Football came easily to me. Football was king. My friends and I lived for the day we'd be seventh graders when we'd be Redhounds. I played football in fifth and sixth grade and waited for seventh grade when I could try out for the school team.

A month before football practice was scheduled to begin, and the summer before my seventh grade, I went blind. Just like that. The bacterial meningitis started with a sledgehammer headache that flamed into a raging fever. My whole body swelled to twice its size; and in the hospital, doctors fought to save my life. They told my frantic parents, "It's doubtful he'll live through the night."

Mom and Dad begged God to spare me. He did, but I awoke to a world as gray as a blown-out TV screen. A sickening grief crunched me like bones breaking. Within days of my first Redhound football practice, I realized that I would never be able to play.

The guys came to visit me in the hospital. "Hey man. How's it going?" That was Zac. Ryan was next to him, and Jerry was fiddling with my food tray. They were shocked at how I recognized their voices. We laughed and talked about the Dallas Cowboys and school and what was going on in town. But we didn't talk about the Redhounds. When it was time for them to go, I listened to their receding footsteps pummeling the linoleum. I knew they were headed for the football field. Practice was about to start.

Seventeen days later I was riding home from the hospital with my parents. That was a miracle since I should have been dead, or at least severely brain damaged. But I was, as the doctor said, "only blind." I asked my parents if we could stop and get a cane. I heard the catch in Mom's voice. "Sure, sure, Travis. You can get anything you want."

When we pulled up to the house, Dad said, "There are friends and neighbors on the lawn, Travis. They're holding a big welcome-home sign." I stumbled out of the car, clutching my new cane. The smell of hot pavement and grass wafted up. I heard voices and foot-steps. It was confusing and I was tired.

"Hey Travis, we decorated your room!"

That was Zack. Stacy, my neighbor from three doors down was on my other side. "Need help, Travis?" she asked shyly. "No, thanks," I said.

I swept my cane in front of me and made it through the front door. Home: clock ticking, refrigerator humming, the feel and smell of the carpet. My friends followed me through to the living room, back down the narrow hall to my bedroom. I remembered it was decorated in the colors of the Redhounds—red and white.

Suddenly balloons hit me in the face. I put up my hands and felt streamers. Everyone was talking at once, just like old times. "You guys are great," I said, overwhelmed.

But that joyous homecoming gave way to hard reality: I had to learn to live all over again. At the Kentucky School for the

Blind, my parents and I learned how to "handle a blind person." Representatives from the school even went to my middle school and talked with the teachers and students. They were helpful, but the hole in my life was football. To be shut out of the team was lonelier than the darkness that surrounded me day and night. I cried out to God but to no one else.

One night, just before school started, Mom and Dad and I went for a drive. The car windows were down and the breeze was cool. Suddenly the wind shifted. "What's that noise?" I asked, already knowing the answer.

Mom sucked in her breath. Dad hesitated. Then he said, "It's the Redhounds practicing, Son. We're passing the football field." I could feel Mom looking at me. I felt her tears and realized this was as hard on them as it was on me. I didn't say anything, but I wanted to die.

That's how badly I missed being one of the guys on the field. No matter how much they included me, I was an outsider unless I could play. And being left out was my biggest fear.

As we drove on, the sounds of football practice faded; but I heard a voice saying, "trust me."

Seventh grade whizzed by. I was in the same school I attended in sixth grade, so I knew the halls, the stairwells, the cafeteria. In class I sat up front. I took tests orally, and I made straight A's. By the end of each day, I was exhausted from thinking about things I used to take for granted. It took a lot of energy just to walk the hall and listen for who was around and where.

The seventh-grade football team went undefeated that season; and they invited me to their banquet where the team presented me with their trophy. I put it on a shelf in my room but couldn't stop hoping for a miracle that would allow me to play football. I could feel myself on the field, could feel the ground under my cleats. I knew I could do it. "God, I'm going to keep trusting you."

It's funny how something can be snatched away so suddenly—

then given back just as suddenly. Near the end of May, Mom picked me up at school. It was a warm day and the windows were down. Horns were blowing; kids were yelling. Through the din, Mom shouted, "I talked with Coach Farris today about your helping with the team."

I slid down in the seat. The only thing I wanted to do was play.

Then Mom said, "Coach wants you to play. "

I couldn't answer. I was afraid I hadn't heard her right. But she said it again and I heard myself yelling, "Yessssssss!"

Summer dragged by. I couldn't wait for football practice to start. I'd lie awake at night and think about being part of the Redhounds, and I thanked God for this chance. Every morning I touched a Bible verse I'd taped above my desk before I went blind. It said: "I can do all things through Christ who strengthens me." I'd need that strength.

On the first day of practice, the guys and I grunted out of the locker room into the steamy August heat with our cleats thudding on the ground. I was sweating from excitement and the weight of the pads. A hand clamped onto my shoulder, and Coach Farris's voice said, "I'm going to be just as hard on you as I am on the others."

"Okay," I said. The last thing I wanted was to be a token member.

I didn't know how hard it would be. After pushups, Coach bellowed and blew the whistle for wind sprints. With a guy on either side of me, I took off. I managed fifty yards. Then I fell, face down in the grass. I got up and fell again. My lungs were on fire. But my ears were filled with cheers from the team and bystanders. "Come on, Travis. You can do it!" And I did. I became center for the Redhounds. God not only gave me back my life when I should have died, he went for the extra point. He gave me back football.

Face to Face

Daniel Zamani

The stagnant desert air felt like a warm blanket wrapped around me. It was probably two in the morning and the soft moonlight illuminated the rustic empty streets. In the distance, mountains jutted up into the sky like stalwart warriors standing guard over the city. But the setting's magnificence faded in the glare of a streetlight reflecting off the gun the man was pointing at me.

It was the summer of 1999 and I was visiting my father's family in Tehran, the capital of Iran. A member of the Basiji, the official morality police, had stopped my taxi. The Basiji were out patrolling the streets because anger over the government's shut-down of several liberal newspapers had caused widespread rioting throughout the city. The riots had lasted three days, with no sign of stopping. I had heard that many people had been severely injured, but somehow I still felt as detached from the unrest occurring all around me as if I had seen it on television.

I had been at my grandparents' house that night reading when I received a call from my cousin, who wanted me to come over so that he could show me a new computer game. I normally would not have made the trip that late, but I was so bored I was looking for any excuse to go out. I left a note for my grandparents and called a taxi to take me to my uncle's house in northern Tehran. I was aware of the dangers of traveling at night and the potential of getting stopped by the Basiji, yet my fear was outweighed by excitement at making the late-night journey.

But fear took over when my taxi was stopped. I studied the person who had ordered me out of the car. He was only a few inches taller than me, but he seemed to loom over me. His bronzed face was covered with dark rudiments of facial hair matching the tousled mass on his head. His black eyes stared at me.

"Show me your wallet!" he barked. I fumbled for my wallet, eager to prove to him that I meant no trouble. I watched nervously as he rifled through it, searching through all of its miscellaneous teenage paraphernalia.

Suddenly, he thrust a small card in front of my face. "What is this?" he demanded. I told him that it was an American library card.

His hand snapped to his gun as he asked why I had such a thing. I replied, "I use it to check out books in California." Apparently, neither the American clothes I was wearing nor my American accent had tipped him off. I wondered what a Basiji member would do to someone who came from the country that they called "The Land of the Great Satan."

It seemed the boy that stood in front of me was not sure what he should do either. He turned slightly, almost imperceptibly; now the barrel of the gun was aimed directly at my chest. Any move, and I felt certain I would feel a volley of bullets tear through my body. We stood, staring uneasily at each other. I prayed silently, making my peace with those I wanted to forgive and with those I wished would forgive me. Yet I vowed not to give up without a fight. I tensed my body, readying myself to jump him. He tightened his grip on the gun and pointed it more decisively at me, looking as if he would fire at any moment. However, as I studied my enemy with his threadbare clothing, the rip in his sandals exposing his dirty feet, the thing I saw most clearly was the frightened look in his eyes. It was obvious that he was just as scared as I was.

Suddenly, an older Basiji member came hurrying over to see what was going on. He began barking questions at me, angrily at first, but when I explained why I was out so late at night, he looked back and forth between the other boy and me, then threw his head back and laughed. We both jumped, startled, which made the man laugh even louder. He said, "Look at the two of you, scared to death of your own shadows! Go home, both of you."

The other boy and I looked at each other again. Then my former interrogator dropped the gun to his side and began to walk away. On impulse, I stopped him and stuck out my hand. He gaped at it, then looked back at my face. I held his gaze and he slowly reached out and grasped my hand. "*Khodahafez,*" I said. "May God protect you." He shook my hand and repeated the word slowly. "*Khodahafez.*"

I got back into the taxi, dazed at how surreal it all had seemed. I couldn't help but think of how close I had come to being killed, and more frightening, how ready I had been to kill another. Yet as my tension slowly eased, I realized how little it had taken for me to see my enemy as a person. Despite the fact that we came from drastically different backgrounds and would probably live drastically different lives, we were both nothing more than frightened children that night. All we needed was a reminder of what made us the same.

In today's world, I feel that all we need is that little reminder, a little bit of understanding to humanize that which is unfamiliar to us.

That is why I will take the time to sit with a homeless person on the streets of San Francisco and talk about our mutual love for the guitar. That is why I will play tag for hours with my friends' younger siblings. That is why I will sit by the bed of my sick grandfather and listen to his stories. That is why I have faith in the human race.

Lost in the Alps

Matt Sanders

The manager of the youth hostel in Zermatt, Switzerland, looked at me like l was crazy. I'd just told him I planned a Christmas Eve trek through the Alps—by myself.

"The snow is waist deep up there on that glacier!" he said. "And there's a bad storm headed this way: typhoon-force winds, sub-zero temperatures."

"Don't worry, I'm in great shape," I assured him. Back at college, I'd been training for marathons. And I'd scaled mountains in Colorado and Wyoming. "Plus, I've got it all planned. Its only a day trip, so I'll be back by dark, before the storm hits."

This was the vacation of a lifetime. Id taken off eight days earlier from Stephen F. Austin University in Texas, where I was a senior. The plan was for me to meet my mom, stepdad, and brother in Milan, Italy, on December 26. We'd celebrate Christmas and my birthday, Dcember 30, touring around Europe. Until then, I had a chance to fulfill my dream of hiking the Alps.

Before dawn the next morning, I double-checked my supplies: a couple packs of dried food, energy bars, and two bottles of water; an extra change of long underwear; a map, my camera, and a headlamp; crampons (metal spikes to wear over my boots when the going got icy); and a climber's ice ax. I decided to throw in my bright orange sleeping bag. Even though I wasn't going to need it, I always liked to be overprepared.

Outside the youth hostel, the thermometer registered a crisp fifteen degrees. A full moon lit my way as I started my climb on a well-used sledding trail through the woods. I pushed hard, sweat drenching my clothes.

By the time the sun came up, I ran out of sledding trails. A hard-packed ski slope lay ahead. Time to use crampons, I thought, opening my backpack and slipping the metal spikes over my boots.

With crampons on, I climbed the mountain, my calves burning with every step. The view was awesome with snowcapped peaks against a backdrop of blue sky.

After about four hours, I reached a train station several miles up the mountain where I ate some oatmeal and filled my water bottle. My next challenge lay just down the slope from the station: Gorner glacier. The glacier was an ice-covered valley I'd have to cross before climbing to a ski gondola on the Breithorn, the huge peak on the other side.

I set out across the glacier; and before long, the snow got deeper. My hips burned after a few steps. "No pain, no gain," I told myself. But as hours passed, I realized I wasn't making much progress. If I don't cross by two o'clock, I vowed, I'll turn back for the train station.

Finally, I reached the far side of the glacier. I stopped to check my watch: two-thirty. I had made it! I was only thirty minutes behind schedule. I pushed myself, climbing the mountain relentlessly; but before I knew it, it started to get dark. I put on my headlamp and checked the map. The gondola station was not far. I climbed a while longer, but the ice was slippery, even with crampons.

Suddenly, I lost my balance. I grappled to regain my footing, and came to a stop only inches before plummeting off a ledge. As my heart pounded, I told myself, "that's your signal to stop."

I found shelter under an outcropping of rock, fired up my stove, and used the last of my fuel to cook some dehydrated noodles. Soaking wet from sweat and snow, I dreaded the thought of spending the night at nine thousand feet. Exhausted, I snuggled into my sleeping bag.

Several hours later, I awoke to what sounded like a roaring jet engine. Snow swirled everywhere, and frigid wind knifed through my sleeping bag, chilling my wet body. I shook uncontrollably, and I couldn't feel my feet. I took off my boots and socks and frantically rubbed my feet, but they stayed numb.

I wrapped my feet in an extra pair of long underwear and cocooned myself in my sleeping bag, cinching the top closed. Thank God I had spent the extra money to get a sleeping bag rated for extreme conditions, I thought. The wind blew in deafening gusts followed by eerie lulls. Lying in the darkness, more scared than I'd ever been, I prayed, "Lord, please help me to get out of here."

Around noon, the storm let up a little and I stuffed my swollen feet into my frozen boots, grabbed my backpack, and set off for the gondola station. Immediately a gust of wind picked me up and threw me four feet. I fought my way through the thigh-deep snow; but after a couple minutes, I couldn't feel my hands. I lurched back to the rock and burrowed deep in my sleeping bag once again. Then I realized that it was Christmas Day.

The growls from my stomach were louder than the howling wind, and my mouth felt like cotton. I had a package of rice, but without gas for my stove, no way to cook it. That left me with three energy bars and an all-you-can-eat snow buffet.

I can't eat snow, I told myself. I'll get hypothermia and freeze to death. Instead, I packed my water bottle with snow and put it in the warmest place available, under layers of clothing next to my stomach. It took six hours to melt down to four ounces of water. My Christmas dinner was half an energy bar and water.

As night fell, I felt isolated, lonely, and completely helpless. I knew if I slept I might never wake up. So I kept myself awake by saying the Lord's Prayer over and over. At noon the next day, the storm still raged. My family would be waiting for me at the rental car counter at the Milan airport. I thought of the e-mail I'd jokingly sent my mother: "Only a natural disaster or accident could keep me from being there on time. So call the U. S. Embassy if I'm not there by noon." Now it wasn't so funny after all, and I knew Mom wouldn't rest until I was safe. She'd send someone to rescue me, somehow.

I forced myself to stay awake all night. I stared at the sheltering rock above me and wondered if it would double as my tombstone.

On my fourth day on the mountain, the wind subsided and I resolved to walk out. I gathered my gear, pulled on my frozen boots, and ate half an energy bar. A few wobbly steps later, I fell to my knees. My legs were too weak.

"Okay Matt, on to Plan Two," I said. "Get to a place where you can be seen." The ridge about two hundred vertical feet away looked like the ideal spot. Dragging my useless body, I crawled up the slope, using my ice ax to pull me along. Two hours later I stood on top of the ridge, supporting most of my weight with the ax.

Suddenly, from out of nowhere, I heard *thrum, thrum, thrum*, the rhythmic beat of helicopter blades. "I'm here!" I cried and waved my sleeping bag.

Tears froze on my cheeks as the helicopter turned and headed back to the village. It was a sightseeing helicopter. Maybe the pilot is going back to tell rescuers where to find me. For an hour I stood on the ridge and waited, but the rescue helicopter never came.

It was warmer now, so I decided to stay on the ridge rather than return to my rock. I found a shallow ditch, grabbed my bag, and sealed myself in.

The next morning, December 28, big black birds flew overhead—a sign that the weather was improving. Some of them perched on a rock near where I lay. I didn't like the way they were looking at me.

"Go away birds. I'm not dead yet!" I shouted. All day I watched sightseeing helicopters come and go, but they were too far away. I could even hear the train and gondola running—so near, but cruelly out of reach. I had to find a way to keep my brain active. So I sang the lyrics to my favorite songs and repeated lines from my favorite movies.

On my sixth day on the mountain, the weather improved. Helicopters, gondola, and the train were running. I even saw skiers in the distance but could only wave feebly. I prayed, not for me, but for my family.

When night fell, I was exhausted. I'd been awake 128 hours. I lay down in my ditch and slept and awoke to a golden sunrise over the most spectacular mountains in the world. It was my birthday, and hope filled my heart. "A guy can ask for anything he wants for his birthday, right?" I asked the heavens. "Well, all I want is a helicopter."

I decided to look for my pack. There it was, just over the ridge. I retrieved it and devoured half of my last energy bar. Then I packed my water bottle with snow.

As the day wore on and my helicopter didn't come, I decided I'd have to leave this place. I might die today, but not on this mountain. I stripped my pack of everything except my water bottle, sleeping bag, crampons, and ice ax. Just as I was preparing to drag myself away in my frostbitten stocking feet, I looked up. *Thrum, thrum, thrum.* A red rescue helicopter was approaching. That sound was more beautiful to me than a chorus of angels singing "Happy Birthday."

I hobbled to the helicopter, blinded by snow and tears. Then I fell to my knees. "Thank you God and thank you, Mom."

As we lifted off, I looked down on the breathtaking, treacherous mountains. I'd made many foolish mistakes, but God hadn't abandoned me. He'd given me the strength to survive seven days in the Alps. And he'd given me a birthday present I'll never forget.

Mountain Lion

Aaron Hall

I t was my idea of the perfect summer job: working as a camp counselor in the Rocky Mountains. I loved the outdoors—I was a Life Scout well on my way to making Eagle. And I loved kids. So when I was offered a position as a counselor at Marshall Mountain day camp, I jumped at the chance.

After a few days on the job, though, I realized working with kids could also be a real pain. During our safety lessons, we tried to tell the kids what to do if they ever got lost or found poison ivy or if they met one of the very few mountain lions that roamed the area.

"If you see a mountain lion," I told them, "don't crouch down or turn your back and run. Just stand tall, wave your arms, and yell at it—really loud. You want to show the cougar that you're not prey, that you are the dangerous one."

The kids giggled and screamed and roared. I had to smile. But I wondered what I'd do myself if I ever ran across a mountain lion. Could I stand my ground?

After a few days, the kids were tired of making bead necklaces and playing games, so two other counselors and I decided it was time to take them up Marshall Mountain for a hike. One hot and sunny morning, we plodded up the trail with about forty campers.

I was at the head of the group, pointing out different birds and trees to the kids. They really had a big time laughing at the bear scat we found. As we walked along, though, something kept bugging me, saying, "Go back, back to the rear."

I shrugged it off. Everything was going well, the kids were keeping up, and one of the other counselors was already back there. We were almost halfway to the top of the mountain.

"Look at that bald eagle," I called out, pointing as it soared above the trees in the bright blue sky. Then the inner voice came again. "Go back. Go back," more insistent than ever.

I know sometimes God gets your attention in mysterious ways. So I decided to listen to the voice. Though it seemed crazy, I turned to another counselor and said, "I'll take over the rear." As I worked my way down to the back of the group, I still wondered what I was doing.

At the rear, I found myself with the littlest ones. Some of them really weren't too interested in climbing. They'd stop for any excuse, like picking up a funny-looking stick. "You'll find much better ones around the bend," I promised, just to keep them moving. Maybe this is why I'm here, to buck up the little ones, I thought. We clambered on as the path got narrower, the trees looming on both sides of us. One kid, Dante Swallow, a cute little guy, trotted behind me at the very end of the line. He was only six, no more than forty pounds, with blonde curly hair.

Every so often he'd say, "Hey, that branch looks like an Indian trail sign" or "Look, I found a lucky rock!"

"You've got good eyes, Dante," I'd yell over my shoulder. Then I heard him say, "Hey, there's a mountain lion!"

I wheeled around. In an instant, a tawny streak exploded from the trees. Before I could even realize what was happening, it slammed little Dante to the ground. Its claws slashed into Dante's T-shirt, leaving bloody gashes on the boy's back. "Oh God!" I gasped. I watched it sink its powerful jaws into Dante's neck.

I spun around to the others, screaming, "Get away!" Shrieks erupted from the kids as they turned to run; the counselors froze.

My anger flared and without thinking, I ran toward the lion, yelling at the top of my lungs. It paid no attention to me as it crouched over Dante. Fear for the boy wiped out my own terror and I found myself charging the animal, kicking its muscular side as hard as I could. I kicked again and again, and I even punched it with all my might. Oh Lord, save Dante, give me strength.

In a fit of rage, I roared and slammed my foot into the cougar's whiskered face. It dropped Dante! My heart lifted, but the animal wheeled and glared at me. So I pulled back to boot it again. It edged back about eight feet and crouched, facing me. I knew a mountain lion could spring ten feet to attack! I had an urge to step back, but I caught myself, remembering my own advice: "Don't run." Yelling, I charged at it. The lion hesitated, then whirled and ran off, its big black tail disappearing in the trees. Breathing thanks to God, I immediately turned to Dante, who lay lifeless, blood from his fang-punctured neck darkening the dust. Picking him up, I tried to stop his bleeding with the bandana I'd been wearing around my neck.

Just then, a maintenance worker who heard the commotion came roaring up in his pickup truck. Another counselor helped me get Dante into the truck and, praying all the way, we took off, racing down the winding trail. We used the truck's radio to call 911, and in five minutes we met the ambulance back at the camp.

Dante suffered severe neck and back wounds, but he survived. A lot of people gave me credit for saving Dante's life, but I believe God put me in the right place at the right time. As a Scout, I still live by the "Be Prepared" motto. But now I understand that means more than wearing the right clothes and carrying the right gear. It means being prepared to really listen when somebody's giving divine directions.

Trapped in the Cave

Michael Ulrich

"hat boy is still trapped!" Dad said. "Gerry, get dressed. You, too, Mike. Maybe we can help."

It was six-thirty in the morning, but right away Gerry and I knew which boy he was talking about. It had been the top news story on radio and TV the night before.

Sixteen boys and three teachers from the Methodist Children's home in Berea, Ohio, had gone on an outing. The van carrying them had broken down shortly before noon. While it was being repaired, three of the young guys spotted a cave and decided to do a little exploring. One of them who was my age—fifteen—crawled through a narrow opening in the cave's interior, then became disoriented and slid headfirst about ten sloping feet into a V-shaped crevice. He was stuck fast.

By mid-afternoon, newscasters had put out a call for help. Volunteers needed to be strong, yet small enough to squeeze into the narrow passage where the boy was trapped.

That night after hearing the news, Dad seemed especially serious. His eyes scanned us eight boys gathered around the supper table, and I wasn't surprised when he said, "We ought to do something."

"They've got plenty of experts and gear," Mother said. "You'd only get in their way."

Dad said nothing more about it until the next morning when he headed for work and heard on his car radio that after eighteen hours, the boy, Morris, was still wedged in the cave.

Rescuers had been working all night. An eighty-five-pound nurse from Akron with ropes tied around her waist, had slithered through the opening and managed to wriggle within two feet of the victim. But she panicked in the cramped quarters and had to be pulled out.

Ohio's governor had contacted expert spelunker William Karras, flying him and his crew in from Washington, D.C., in an Air Force jet. But even Mr. Karras—135 pounds and skinny as a piece of spaghetti—wasn't thin enough to get through to hook rescue gear onto Morris. A rig was being brought to drill down a hundred feet from the top of the overlying cliff. It was a dangerous move—the whole cave might collapse. But all other efforts had failed.

That's when Dad pulled up to a phone booth and reported he wouldn't be at work. And he turned around and came back home to get us kids.

An hour later, he and Gerry and I had driven the twenty miles to Wildcat Cave. You would have thought a county fair was going on. Reporters, cars, people were everywhere. Generators kept the lights and equipment going. The opening of the cave itself looked like a huge, dark mouth waiting for its next victim.

Dad asked to see someone in charge; he said maybe we could help. But so many others had volunteered that no one paid much attention to us.

Mr. Karras was pacing and running his fingers through his hair. Dad looked at us and when we nodded our okay, he tapped Karras's shoulder.

"I'm sure my boys can squeeze through. They're small, but they're tough."

Mr. Karras studied us. You could tell he was desperate. Finally he said, "You'll have to sign a liability release." Dad hesitated, swallowed, then uncapped his pen.

Gerry was twelve years old and weighed only eighty-two pounds. Mr. Karras attached two ropes to my brother, gave him a light and plenty of instructions. Morris was trapped about ten feet down in a crack about eighteen inches wide at the top and nine inches at the bottom.

We watched Gerry wiggle through a slit in one of the cave's inside walls. Almost right away he yelled he wanted out and was hauled back. "Did you get to him?" we shouted.

"Almost." Gerry was pale. "But I can't do it!" He bent over, sick.

"Okay, son," Dad said, hugging Gerry. Mike, It's your turn."

My usual weight was 135, but I had trained down to 120 to get on the high-school wrestling team. Dad also told Mr. Karras about my first-aid training as an Eagle Scout.

I worked my way through the darkness like a crab, while the others shone lights in behind me. I eased to the fissure headfirst, wriggling downward in a weird kind of swim. The passageway was so tight I had to exhale in order to inch myself ahead. Every time I took a breath, I was locked tight against the wall.

Minutes later I had squirmed my way only eight feet. No wonder the kid got stuck in here. I could get caught myself.

When I finally got close to Morris, I understood why my brother had gotten sick. Morris smelled like a rotten fish. he had been pinned in twenty hours by then. The odor turned my stomach too.

Rescuers above were poking lights in as far as they could. But I was in my own shadow. I couldn't use my right hand, either. I needed it to brace myself to keep from sliding in on top of Morris.

"Get me out," I heard him say, "please." He couldn't help me. One arm was wedged beneath him. Worse, he was slipping in and out of consciousness.

Mr Karras's voice echoed through the opening. He was yelling at Morris about how stupid he was to have gone in the cave in the first place. It was a smart tactic. It roused the trapped boy, making him mad enough to answer, "When I get out of here, I'm going to beat you up!" Anger made his blood stir, keeping him alert.

With my left hand I worked a strap around one of his knees. The hardest part was getting it through the buckle using only one hand.

Sucking in my breath, I wriggled back out. Mr. Karras and the other rescuers cheered and grabbed the ropes to pull at Morris's body.

My limbs felt as if they were full of hot needles. I rubbed them to get feeling back. Wrestling had never taken strength like that! It was good to see daylight again, to breathe in fresh air instead of a stale cave and a kid who smelled like an outhouse.

The cheering stopped. It turned out the pulling had merely wedged Morris tighter.

"Not enough lift," Mr. Karras announced. He looked at me, still sprawled on the ground. "You're the boy's only hope," he said. "I hate to ask you, but could you go in again?"

When he said that, the story of David and Goliath flashed across my mind. This was a challenge that sure seemed as big as any Goliath. David had been a young guy like me. And he had been given strength to conquer his giant. With God's help, I would, too.

It was even harder the second trip in. But at least I had been given more directions about what to do.

I attached another strap; this one around both of Morris's legs. Next, I groped the rocks to find someplace to hook on a second rope. A doorknob-sized stone jutting out might work. With my left hand—and my teeth—I fastened a loop around the rock to pass the first rope through, like a pulley—to give lift.

When I finally got out, I couldn't stand without help. The men hauled on the rope. "It's working!"

Then groans again. Only the bottom half of Morris was

moving. His upper half was still stuck fast.

Nobody said anything. Mr. Karras's eyes were moist as he came toward me again. I shouldn't be asked to make another trip into that pit.

I bet David had felt weak, scared, not up to the task. And in the Bible story he had carried five stones—not just one or two—when he went to face Goliath. As I saw it, he had intended to persevere, not just turn and run if his first attempt didn't hit its mark. He had a job to do and he did it.

So I began my third trip into that cold, dark dungeon. Once again I made a loop of rope with my left hand and teeth. Morris was barely conscious. "You've got to help me or you'll never be able to get out and beat up Mr. Karras," I told him. That roused him and finally, between us, we worked the rope around and beneath his shoulders.

I secured the ropes and straps—for the last time, I hoped. Then I slowly shimmied back out again.

This time the rescue team had rigged up a long pole with a hose attached. They shoved it into the crack, then poured a gallon of glycerin into the hose. Morris was greased like a pig to help slide him out.

The men pulled. Morris moved. He was emerging! At 1:30 that afternoon I got my first real look at the boy I had helped save. Bruises covered his face. Morris was carried to a waiting ambulance. After more than twenty-five hours of being trapped, he was free. "He'll be fine in a few days," doctors said.

Suddenly I was no longer tired. I felt good. Sometimes the tasks or circumstances we face seem like Goliaths. They appear to be impossible. But when you confront them, you'll be given the strength to carry on, overcome—and maybe even help somebody else along the way.

Terror on the Ice

Jack Frantz

now sprayed from our snowmobiles as we glided through patches of swirling fog with the fifteen-degree air freezing our breaths. My twelve-year-old brother, Brower, sat beind me on the sled my dad was pulling. Uncle Dan and Dad's cousin, Leonard, were right behind us on their snowmobiles.

We were all on a big offshore ice field in the open ocean, ten miles outside of Barrow, Alaska's northernmost city. Part of our Inuit Eskimo tradition was to welcome the annual migration of the mysterious Eider ducks to their Arctic summer grounds, and we were out here to do just that. Of course, my father looked forward to getting a couple of the birds for dinner. My grandmother loved duck.

We started out about nine in the evening, but during this time of year, there was daylight almost around the clock. It was May, and Dad said the ice pack should be safe. Still, we had prayed for protection; in our part of the world there are no guarantees.

As I squinted into the murky light, sky and water merged into a ghostly haze. I thought about the Barrow whalers on their annual hunt with harpoons, skin boats, and skinning tools, and who were camped on this same ice some ten miles away. We knew some of them and hoped they would have a good catch. Their families depended on their success.

Soon giant ice hummocks loomed before us. "Can't cross those ridges on these machines," Leonard called. "You and the boys walk on ahead. Dan and I will watch the machines."

So Dad, Brower, and I set out, pulling a blue plastic sled loaded with snacks and extra clothes. After awhile we saw the dark blue Chukahi sea surging against the ice a few hundred yards ahead. "We'll see some ducks soon, boys," Dad called.

Suddenly, a cracking sound made us stop and look behind us. The hair on the back of my neck shot straight up as a dark ribbon of open sea zigzagged across the path we'd taken. The ice was breaking up! As we watched, the crack widened and the powerful sea surged beneath the ice we were on.

"Dad!" I yelled, running toward the crack. "Should we jump?"

He shook his head and waved us back. Dark stretches of seawater had opened all around us. We were trapped on an ice floe!

Would the raging sea shatter the ice beneath us? By now the fog had closed in and smothered us in white nothingness.

"Dad, we're drifting out to sea," cried Brower.

"Don't worry," I said, "Dad's gonna figure something out." I sure hoped I was right.

"Boys, stand back," Dad warned. "I'm going to signal Dan and Leonard." He aimed his twelve-gauge shotgun high and fired three rounds. The sound was swallowed up in the thick mist.

I shivered and looked around. The ice floe on which we stood was only about 200 by 100 yards. It could break apart any second.

Dad saw the panic in our eyes and gathered us close, his strong arms around our shoulders. "Boys, we must trust in God," he said. "If we do our best, he will see us through this." Then he asked God to help us. "Lord, help us to know what to do. Please keep us safe."

All we could do was swallow hard and hug him back.

Then Dad mentioned the whalers. "Boys, let's pray for them,

too," he said. We knelt on the ice and asked God to keep them safe.

My heart rose as I saw Dad pull his new cell phone from his parka.

"I'll call Barrow Search and Rescue," he said, "and give them our position."

"But how will the pilots see us in this fog?" asked Brower.

"We'll build a fire," Dad replied.

"With what?"

"The sled. The plastic will burn some." Dad began slashing the sled into strips with his knife, making a small pile of plastic.

"You two cover this with anything that'll burn while I call for help." he ordered.

Brower and I quickly scrounged up stuff like boxes, old sweats, and a cardboard soft drink carton. I wondered if our fire would be bright enough to be seen in this thick fog.

Suddenly, Dad stopped talking on his cell phone. I glanced up to see a frown cross his face. He was shaking the phone and pressing buttons. "What happened, Dad?" I asked, fear squeezing me.

"Nothing to worry about, guys," he said. "Let's make sure that fire will be bright enough." He took a couple of shotgun shells, pried them open, and poured the gray gunpowder onto our little fire.

"With so little fuel we won't light it until we hear aircraft overhead," he said. "Now we'll just sit tight until they come."

He sounded so confident. But it was awful just waiting, hearing the ominous creaks and groans as chunks of ice crumbled off the edge of our floe. It was close to midnight now, and even though this was a time of year when we have sunlight almost twenty-four hours a day, the fog had pretty much blocked out the sun.

As time dragged, I remembered hearing stories of snowmobiles being carried out to sea on floes just like this one, never to be seen again. I worried about Dad's phone call. Had he gotten through?

Two hours later, I heard a whopping sound in the distance.

"Dad, a chopper," I yelled. We all jumped up. Dad lit a match and dropped it on the kindling. The gunpowder flared white-hot, and soon the fire was crackling. But, as we held our breaths, the helicopter noise drifted away and disappeared.

"They didn't see us," I groaned, slumping down on the ice.

"They'll be back," Dad said. "Come on, we've got to keep this fire going."

We scrambled together some more pieces of clothing and scraps of paper and tossed them on the smoking embers. Then Brower and I huddled together. I felt sorry for the times I used to yell at him for bugging me. "Listen, you two. Listen like foxes," called Dad.

"Yeah, Dad, we're listening," I mumbled.

Listen to what, I wondered. The fire was down to a smolder.

The pounding of a helicopter made me jump up. "Dad, it's near us." We all looked up but couldn't see a thing in the fog.

Dad grabbed a pair of sweatpants and threw them on the embers. I held my breath, afraid they would put out the fire. Instead, brilliant orange flames shot high in the air.

Soon the chopper thundered right over us. We could make out its dark shape, and we yelled and waved. I could hear Dad praying. "O Lord, let the ice hold."

Browser was going nuts, running for the helicopter and yelling, "They found us! They found us!" And I was right behind him. Dad shouted for us to be careful as he followed us across the ice. The men in the helicopter hauled us all inside and we lifted off.

"We were about to head back to base," one of the crew members said. "Then we saw a glow in the murk. That was some fire you had going." Looking down, I saw our fire had dwindled to nothing. Dark cracks ran all through our ice floe. Another few minutes and we'd have been gone.

As Dad grabbed Brower and me in a big hug, I choked "I knew you'd get us out of there, Dad."

"No, Son," he said. "God got us out of there."

Off Track

Liz Toman

A patchwork of corn and alfalfa fields rushed past my window as I drove home from track practice. My father and his father have farmed this land, I thought with pride. I had learned to love these fields, too, not from the seat of a tractor, but from inside my running shoes with my dog at my side.

Running was everything to me. This year, my senior year in high school, I ws among Canada's best junior track and field athletes. I'd won every heptathlon I'd competed in, become the Ontario champion in numerous events and even had a medal from the Olympic trials last spring. It was early fall, and already I had a pile of college brochures on my desk. Recruiters from Rice, Washington State, Iowa State, and Southern Illinois all wanted me.

I turned into our driveway. "Hi, Mom, hi, Dad," I said as I jumped out of the car, then rolled through the kitchen, grabbing supper on the way. Upstairs, I finished my homework and settled into bed. It had been a long day.

As I turned over, I felt something strange: a lump on the left side of my abdomen. "Maybe it's something everyone has; there's probably one on each side" I thought. I poked at my right side. Nothing. I tried to calm my pounding heart. I would ask about it at my physical next week. "Please, God, don't let it be anything bad," I prayed.

A few days later, my doctor confirmed my worst suspicions. There was definitely something there that shouldn't be. I was referred to a specialist, who tried to reassure me. "Some young women develop harmless growths on their ovaries," he explained. "Yours will have to be removed, but it shouldn't be a major problem."

A week later I underwent the surgery. After I woke up from the anesthesia, the specialist came in. "Liz, I have good news and bad news," he said.

"Bad news first, please."

"The growths were cancerous, Liz," he said softly. "You have ovarian cancer. It's very rare in women your age. We had to remove your left ovary because it had been taken over by a tumor the size of a small football, and we had to take most of your right ovary as well."

"So what's the good news?"

"As far as we can tell, the cancer was contained."

My hands shook as I tried to stay calm. This wasn't supposed to be serious. I took a deep breath. "How long before I can get back on the track?"

His eyebrows shot up. "I tell people six weeks to recover from the surgery you just had. In the meantime I'll share your file with an oncologist. He'll probably want to schedule you for chemotherapy treatments."

The specialist told me some other things; and I nodded as though I were listening, but nothing registered. It was all so surreal. I was about to enter the world of doctors and needles. A feeling of dread set in, but I tried to shake it off. I won't let this set me back, I thought. I'd managed my life perfectly so far. I was a top student and a star athlete. I was involved at school and church. I'll just have to work harder. I'll meet my goals, cancer or no cancer.

Three weeks later, I laced up my running shoes and drove to track practice. My coach met me at my car. "What are you doing here, Liz?"

71

"Working out, what else?"

He shook his head and didn't say much. But he kept a watchful eye on me during practice. If I were going to get a university education, I needed to be ready for those recruiters. I went to work, clearing hurdle after hurdle.

The reality of my situation hit again on a gray Sunday evening a few months later, when I packed for my first week of chemo. Looking around my bedroom, I debated what to bring along for my week-long hospital stay. Medals and trophies decorated the walls and dresser. Piles of textbooks and shiny college brochures crowded my desk. I slipped the brochures into my suitcase.

The next morning as my sister drove me to the hospital, the winter sky and barren fields dampened my spirits even more.

I was determined to rebound quickly from the chemo treatments. I surprised my oncologist by using the hospital treadmill early that week, and I kept busy with visitors and books. My homeroom class brought me a six-foot-long, get-well banner and a basket of gifts. My father came to my room every evening after he got off work and sat by my bed late into the night.

As the week dragged on, the chemo really started to wear me down. I was constantly tired and felt so sick to my stomach that I refused just about every bit of food they brought me. At the end of the week, I remembered the recruitment brochures, athletic information, scholarship packages, dorm-life pamphlets, and course offerings that sat neatly in my suitcase. Hot tears started to roll down my cheeks. My future seemed empty and uncertain.

"God," I prayed, "all my plans are ruined. I don't know what will happen to me after this. I don't know if I'll every compete again, or ever be the best again." Then, among the beeping hospital machines, maze of tubes, and IV drips, a calm came over me. I felt like God was holding me close and telling me, "Don't worry, Liz. I'll take care of you."

In that moment of peace, I realized that I had been wrapped up in my success, my problems, and my future. I wanted to control everything that happened in my life. Even with God I'd been a control freak, demanding to know the plan.

"God, I had big plans," I prayed. "But your plans are bigger. I trust you with everything."

I closed my eyes and slept more soundly that I had in days.

I went through two more rounds of chemo in the next two months. I lost my appetite, my strength, and my hair. But I never lost the peace that God gave me that night in the hospital bed. He was truly my support and strength, my best friend.

During my treatment and recovery, I went back to the track as much as I could, pushing myself to maintain the levels of skill and fitness I had before this all started. I also contacted several of the schools that had been recruiting me, and many were still interested. After visiting Colorado State University, I fell in love with the school and knew it would be my home for the next four years. That spring, I signed papers for a full track and field scholarship and officially became a CSU Ram.

By the grace of God I have stayed cancer-free since my diagnosis and treatment. I won meets and conference championships for the Rams and placed second in the discus at the NCAA championships my senior year. All of this has brought me into the public eye a few times, when I've been intereviewed in newspaper articles or called on to give speeches. Every time someone asks me about my accomplishments, I tell them about my struggles, and how my faith has been strengthened.

I still like making big plans and working hard to accomplish them. But my cancer experience has taught me an important lesson: I'm not in control. Things may not go according to my plan. But that's totally okay with me. God is the one guiding my life and keeping me on track.

Killer Bees

Joe Portale

Our van bounced violently over the rutted dirt road. As I peered through the dust-caked windshield, my stomach growled. I glanced at my watch. We needed to find a spot for lunch, some shade in this desolate country.

I was leading a group of teens and young adults, including several nurses, on a mission to the outback of the West African country of Burkina Faso. Our small caravan was on its way to the bush village of Bouroum Bouroum. There were no other vehicles on the road—a fact that made me even more anxious to reach our destination.

I was tired of traveling. We had come thousands of miles and crossed the Sahara by following tall posts in the sand that marked the route. Now we bounced over a washboard trail on the parched African savanna. Dust was everywhere. When the windshield broke on one van, we had to wear thick bandannas around our mouths just to breathe.

Baobab trees studded the horizon—strange, dreary trees that looked as if they had sprouted upside down, with their gnarled and twisted branches stabbing the sky.

"Let's stop," I said, spotting a large baobab ahead. Here was about as much shade as we'd find. Red dust billowed up as the van jerked to a halt. Everyone got out and stretched, and a group set out our lunch. Lidia, a pretty dark-haired girl, spread old green army blankets on the ground.

While the rest of the group ate, I studied our surroundings. The air seemed oddly still. Cicadas buzzed. I thought I heard a dove coo in the brush. A grasshopper jumped across the blanket, scurrying for cover. Along our route there had been times when I sensed God watching over us. Once, we had managed to find our way in a blinding sandstorm. At a desert oasis we had arrived just in time to help a Bedouin woman who almost died in childbirth. I felt especially close to God while camping in the Sahara beneath the brilliant stars; but now he seemed so far away. This place was too hot, too quiet, too empty. I had a strange feeling of unrest.

"We've got to get going," I announced. We had many more miles to travel, and I was growing impatient. Everyone stood and gathered the blankets. Several of the girls filed behind the tree for a bathroom break.

Suddenly a piercing shriek came from behind the baobab. I sprinted over. A thick buzzing sound filled the air. All at once, a dark menacing cloud appeared: bees! They attacked my ankles and swooped under my collar. They found every inch of my exposed skin. I closed my eyes and tried to brush them away. I slapped at my neck. A hot stinger pierced my cheek, and pain shot through my elbow. I flailed my arms. These were killer bees!

I ran blindly. Anywhere to get away from the deadly, angry roar. I beat the air. The bees kept coming at me, stinging, buzzing. I couldn't tell which way to turn. Trapped by the assault, I hardly dared open my eyes. All around me people were running and screaming. I grabbed one girl by the arm and pulled her away from the baobab tree. The bees near her attacked my face. We dashed up the road, waving our arms, trying to outrun the cloud. My feet pounded the dirt as I ran away from the terrible noise. Several guys carried a girl to us and laid her on the ground. It was Lidia. Everyone gathered around her. She was covered with bees. They were on her eyelids, in her ears, on her arms and hands. Bees buzzed in her long hair.

"I . . . can't . . . breathe," she gasped.

"Hang in there," one of the nurses said as she removed dozens of stingers from the girl's body. Several others helped. Lidia's eyes rolled back and her head fell into the dust of the roadway. I dropped to my knees. I wanted to pray, but my thoughts were jumbled and no words came. I felt only fear and loneliness in this place. Forcing myself, I closed my eyes and spoke, "God, this isn't your fault. Your world is good and beautiful." I couldn't believe my ears. The words were coming automatically. I was thanking God for his whole creation. His whole creation even in the midst of this disaster. But something told me it was the right prayer. "Thank you, God, for these bees," I prayed. "They are a part of your world. You are gracious and good." I opened my eyes. The wild buzzing had diminished. We picked stingers out of our skin. Bees still swarmed around our van as though searching for their hive.

"We've got to get medicine," one of the nurses called. She knew there was some in the van. She stood up from the dust. "I'll go," she said.

We watched as she staggered back, waving her arms. Darting into the van, she grabbed a medical kit. She ran back to Lidia and gave her a shot of antihistamine. "I don't think she's going to make it," someone said.

"Thank you, Lord, for your creation," I continued to pray. "For all your creatures. Thank you for life."

One of our drivers covered himself with blankets and ran back to the vans. Opening the doors so the bees could fly out, he started one van and drove it to us. The van rocked from one side of the road to the other as he jerked the steering wheel to get the angry bees out.

"Thank you, God . . . "

We chased the last of the bees out of the van and lowered Lidia's limp form on the back seat while drivers went for the other vehicles. I sat in front to keep an eye on her and one of the nurses sat next to her and bathed her forehead with a cool, damp cloth. It would be several hours of rough driving before we reached the missionary infirmary. An hour down the road, Lidia stirred. Jerking her arm toward her hair, she mumbled "Cut my hair off."

"It's okay, Lidia. We've pulled the bees out of your hair." Her eyes opened. "Where am I?"

"You're in a van on your way to Bouroum Bouroum," I said.

She leaned weakly on one elbow. "I couldn't breathe. I felt my life leaving me. And I thought, no, Lord, that's not fair to my parents. When you began praying, a cool breeze swept over me and I was able to breathe again."

I wondered how she had heard me praying when she was unconscious. After two-and-a-half hours on the road we arrived at the village, covered with red, swollen welts. We blurted out our story to the missionaries there.

"You are very fortunate," one of them told me as others tended to the most seriously injured. "Not long ago another foreigner disturbed a hive of bees. He was stung more than forty times and died."

That night I fell into my sleeping bag, exhausted. I kept playing the day over in my mind, how we had survived in this hot, dry, lonely land. Just then I felt thin grains of sand between my toes—the dust was as inescapable as God's mercy.

"Thank you, God," I prayed. "Thank you for the dust, the trees, the sand, the wind, the sun, the water, the bees. Your creation is full of mystery and goodness. But your mercy is mightiest of all."

Dear God,
let me soar in the face of the wind;
up—
up—
like the lark,
so poised and so sure,
through the cold
on the storm
with wings to endure.
Let the silver rain wash
all the dust from my wings,
let me soar
as he soars,
let me sing
as he sings;
let it lift me
all joyous
and carefree
and swift,
let it buffet
and drive me
but, God,
let it lift!

RUTH BELL GRAHAM

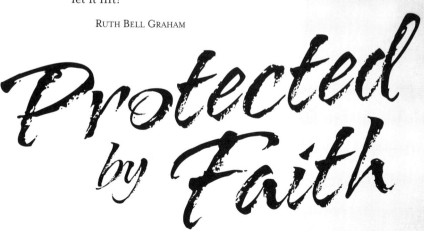

Front-Row Seat

Dwayne Douglas

My father was as sturdy and steadfast as the craggy West Virginia hills where we lived; and like most sons, I viewed him as indestructible. So his death, when I was a teen, struck me with a terrible blow, particularly because I was convinced that I was responsible.

Dad was a lathe operator at a brass foundry, whose ear-splitting whistle we could hear at quitting time even though it was in the next town over. He came home from work soot-smeared and sweaty, brass chips glinting in his dark hair. After a shower he claimed his humble throne—a worn recliner in the family room—until Mom called us to supper. He never talked much until dessert, he was usually so hungry. But then he laughed and joked with my brother, Dana, and me, and helped us with our homework while Mom cleaned up the dishes.

Dad hadn't gone far in school himself. Hard times forced him into the factory. But he had high hopes for his boys. He told me to reserve a front-row seat for him at graduation. It was going to be as big a day for him as it would be for me.

I loved Dad. As hard as he worked, he always drove me to football practice and cheered at Friday-night games. Afterward Dad would throw his arm around me and say, "I'm proud of you, Dwayne," no matter if we had won or lost. One area where we differed, though, was religion. Dad was a true believer. Not that I didn't believe in God, but I was uncertain about the strength of my faith. I didn't lean on my faith the way Dad did. I didn't have much use for church.

One day during my senior year, Dad invited me along while he did some errands after work. "I'll drive us to Martinsburg, then you can take over on the way back." I had just gotten my permit and was thrilled about any chance to practice my driving.

When we started for home, traffic was light. Dad laid a hand on my forearm and said, "I'm proud of you, Son." Then he leaned back, a little like the way he relaxed in his easy chair. I hit a sharp curve. I don't remember what happened after that.

I woke up in an emergency room, a doctor leaning over me intently. "How's my dad?" I gasped. I think I tried to get up.

A nurse said, "I'm sorry, Dwayne, he didn't make it."

Over and over my mother said, "Dwayne, you mustn't blame yourself." But every day I wished it had been me instead of him.

I missed the funeral. I came home to the season's last few leaves drifting like parachutes onto our green roof. The house seemed so empty without him. Through a window, the dusty afternoon light suffused his chair, just as he left it. I stared at the impression his head had left after years of his leaning back. Empty, empty, empty.

I glanced at a sympathy card on the table: "And God shall wipe away all tears." If only it were true.

Somehow I got through my senior year. Three new friends kind of adopted me, and invited me to a Friday-night youth group at their church. I couldn't bring myself to go at first, but soon I gave in to the idea of asking God to help me forgive myself. Where else could I turn but to where Dad had turned?

Then came graduation. Save me a front-row seat, he had said. When my name was called, I hurried, with my head down, across the stage. Before I reached the table where the diplomas were arrayed, I slowed down. A tide of good feeling surged through me, a relief and well-being such as I had never felt before. Then I experienced a kind of glow throughout, a sensation of healing, peace, love, acceptance, and joy. I knew it was God, my heavenly father, wrapping me in forgiveness and reassurance so that I could forgive myself.

I looked out into the audience and half expected to see Dad done up in his Sunday suit with his hair slicked back and applauding until his palms were red. I saw Mom and Dana, beaming. And although I didn't see my father, I felt his love, as indestructible as the West Virginia hills. I knew that he had gotten his front-row seat after all.

Last Wish

Christi Galloway

Chris Hart was not your average sixteen-year-old. He was six feet, eight inches tall and weighed 260 pounds. In his freshman year of high school he played on the varsity football team; he could bench-press 250 pounds and squat 450. Then he was diagnosed with osteogenic sarcoma, a form of cancer. For awhile it was in remission, then during his junior year the cancer returned. A couple of months before Christmas in 1993 he was told by doctors that he probably did not have long to live.

That same year a local radio station sponsored a contest granting requests to people who wrote in with the best Christmas wishes. A member of our church wrote a letter to the radio station on Chris's behalf. Little did I know that when this letter was chosen my world would change too.

Chris's first wish was to have a stereo system for his truck. A local electronics firm obliged. His second wish was to see a Dallas Cowboys football game. That was his favorite team and he was their greatest fan. To his surprise, he not only got to see the Cowboys play, he actually met some of them in the locker room. Chris's third wish was more difficult to coordinate because of its sensitive nature. He wanted a date with a redhead.

At this point I should explain that I am a redhead. My dad came home from church one night and told me about Chris and his three wishes, especially his third wish.

"Dad, I don't even know the guy," I said. How could I go on a date with him? I didn't go to his school. I had never met him. My dad, who is a minister, had visited Chris several times and all he could say about him was that he was very nice, very tall and "big-boned." With some hesitation I said yes.

The date was scheduled for the week before Christmas. Before then Chris and I had only talked on the phone. He seemed sweet, but I was nervous about going out on a date so I asked one of my best friends to join us. When Chris came to pick me up I was a little shocked by how he looked. He was huge, and bald from his chemotherapy treatments. He wore a hat, but took it off inside to be polite, exposing his hairless head. When we went to a local pizza restaurant, he had to duck to get through the door and everybody stared at us.

After that he started to come to my house after school and we talked or watched movies. He told me how much he missed playing football and sometimes we listened to music.

On Valentine's Day a friend and I cooked a special dinner for her boyfriend and Chris. We exchanged presents. Chris seemed pleased with the teddy bear and the new CD. He even asked me to go to his junior-senior prom.

Then I did something I'm still ashamed of. The town newspaper did an article about Chris's three wishes accompanied by a picture of the two of us in front of his truck. The caption said we dated. When kids from school saw the article and picture they made comments. I tried to ignore them, but one day one of the popular seniors said to me, "Hey, I guess that guy couldn't find anybody better to date." It really hurt. I was only a sophomore and still felt new to the town. I wanted people to like me. I didn't want them to think I was weird.

When Chris called, I said I was busy and couldn't talk. I made excuses, so he stopped coming over and we stopped going out. At night I cried myself to sleep because I knew I was being cruel, but I couldn't help it. Chris's prom was coming up and I knew I had to talk to him. So I called Chris and we made plans to go out to dinner with friends before the prom.

That night when he came to pick me up, we didn't talk much at first. He looked good in his tuxedo and sneakers (he couldn't find any black shoes big enough to fit). He had lost a lot of weight. His class ring was so loose it kept falling off.

We joined our friends for dinner and started to laugh and joke like old times. On the way to the dance, Chris began to feel bad. We waited in the parking lot until he regained his strength.

The auditorium was beautifully decorated with an Egyptian theme. Everyone else was dancing and having a great time, but Chris still felt weak, so he could only sit and watch. While we were talking, the DJ interrupted the music and one of the football players took the microphone. He talked about Chris and how special he was. Then they dedicated the prom to Chris and gave him a plaque. It was one of his proudest moments.

After the prom, I didn't care what people at my school thought. They could say whatever they wanted. Chris was my friend. I just hoped he could forgive me for the way I had treated him. That spring he became much worse and the doctors gave him two weeks to live. Every day for those two weeks I visited him. He had a huge bed set up in his bedroom with a lot of pillows, and together we watched television and talked.

He wasn't afraid to talk about dying. I found it painful but my dad said that just by listening to Chris I was helping him.

Each day it got harder for Chris to concentrate. In his last few days he could barely recognize anybody. Saturday afternoon was the last time I got to visit Chris. As I was leaving he called me back and asked for a hug. As I hugged him, he whispered, "I love you." It was the first time he had said those words to me. He really had forgiven me.

Sunday morning I went straight home after church. My parents had suggested I join them at a restaurant for lunch, but I felt there was some reason I shouldn't. Only moments after I got home a phone call came from Chris's dad; Chris was dying. I called the restaurant where my parents were eating and they rushed home and took me to Chris's.

Family and friends were gathered around Chris's bed. He was breathing with great gasps, very slowly. I stood there, but could say nothing. Words wouldn't come.

"Christi's here," my dad said softly. "We're all here and we love you."

"Dear God," my dad prayed, "please be with Chris and all of those present and his family. Give us a sense of peace as you receive Chris into your loving arms."

I looked up to see Chris take his last breath. He was gone.

That was two years ago, and I still miss Chris. I miss the good times we had telling stories, listening to music, laughing, and just being together. I miss him during football season because I know how much that sport meant to him. I miss the sweetness he showed me. He helped my faith grow, for he taught me that friends, no matter what they look like, are truly important.

My dad says that people who show you the love of Christ are "God with skin on." That was Chris.

My Father's Promise

Kenneth Proctor

I sat on the doorstep, my red face wet with tears, and watched my father's car drive away, revealing a familiar empty place. I wanted to say something. I opened my mouth but nothing came out. I was angry and confused, but the firm embrace of my mother's arms rescued me. She had wiped away too many tears, too many times during the preceding years.

That night the opening of the front door awoke me. Footsteps stumbled across the tile floor of our kitchen. Daddy was home; I knew he was drunk. He moved toward my doorway. My father, believing I was asleep, knelt next to my bed. The smell of alcohol burned my nose and caused tears to rise in my throat, but I knew it wasn't the time to cry. The silence in that room seemed to last for years. My father was trying to say so many things. He was trying to express his love. He was trying to tell me how much I meant to him, how I was more important to him than the alcohol on his breath.

"I'm sorry . . . I'm sorry." His words were so quiet yet they filled the entire room. I could feel eyes full of pain staring into my face. "I'm sorry, Son." The tears returned to my throat, but I could not cry. I could not let him know I was awake, that I had heard. My father left my room a few moments later, turning the kitchen light off on his way to bed. I opened my eyes in the darkness and the tears came. I cried that night not only for myself, but also for my family. "Lord," I said that name with so much hope. "Lord, help my family. Lord, help my baby sister; help her not to hurt, not to cry like me. Lord, help Mommy, please help Mommy. Lord, help Daddy be my daddy." That night in my room the Lord promised me that he would bring my daddy back to me. I believed.

For two years these scenes repeated themselves. My mom would send me to my aunt's house while she worked all day. After work, my mother would be exhausted but never too tired to greet me with a joyful embrace. The ride home was always filled with discussion about the day's adventures. I loved talking with my mother; she made me feel like a friend more than a child. But the joy of our car ride home would often be spoiled by a new six-pack on the kitchen counter. I hated everything about those bottles: their unseen hands holding my father, their unheard voices ridiculing me. To me the bottles were the most evil things the world had ever known. I wished I could sit on that counter forever, claiming it as mine. Maybe then there would be no place for the beer, and it would feel unwanted and leave forever.

During those two years I continued to pray for my family. I prayed for strength, help, and happiness. I prayed that God would take away the beer. I prayed every prayer that I could think to pray. I kept believing the Lord would bring my daddy back to me like he had promised.

Gradually I noticed the six-packs of beer on the kitchen counter grow fewer and fewer. My father's devotion to alcohol was abandoned in the wake of his newfound devotion to his family. The Lord had answered my prayer. For the first five years of my life my father was a drunk. He drank away his past and his son. In August 1989, my father entered a program for alcoholics, and has not had a drink since then. The Lord gave me my father, and alcohol will never take him back.

Riding Shotgun
Matt Knutson

"Shotgun!" my friend Fletcher yelled as the three of us raced toward my car one December Friday after school. He hopped victoriously into the coveted passenger seat of my LeBaron, while Curtis threw his book bag into the back and grudgingly climbed in. "Next time I'll ride shotgun," Curtis said. "You wait." The battle between those two was a given whenever I drove.

Once overhearing them, my mom told us that the "shotgun" position went back to stagecoach days, when a man armed with a shotgun sat beside the driver to protect him from bandits. I wasn't sure how much protection Fletcher or Curtis provided, but it was a fun game anyway.

"This time tomorrow we'll be in snowboarding heaven," Curtis said, unzipping his jacket and sprawling out in the back seat. The three of us went snowboarding nearly every Saturday in winter. We'd all grown up in western Montana and couldn't get enough of the mountains. Our weekly trip to Big Mountain was on—no matter what the conditions. And the nastier the weather, the better the snowboarding.

"Let it snow!" Fletcher remarked. "It's really coming down," Curtis said. We always hang out together the night before a trip; but my girlfriend had rented a couple of movies, so I begged off. I dropped the guys off, and promised to pick them up the next day at seven.

By the time I got to Allison's, the plowed driveway was already covered with a new layer of snow. Light, fluffy flakes dusted my car and the path leading up to her porch.

"Are you sure you're going to be all right driving home in this later?" she asked, poking her head out the front door. I glanced at the inch of snow on the path. Allison had grown up in Texas and Saudi Arabia; I explained that this was a typical Montana winter. "I've driven in stuff ten times worse," I said, which was true. "It's just snow."

Allison put the first tape in the VCR, but I could tell she was still worried. "My car handles well, even on slippery roads," I assured her. "Now let's just watch the movie." I sat next to her on the couch and for awhile we forgot about the weather.

After the second movie ended, Allison looked out the window. "Dad can give you a ride, Matt," she said. I protested. "Then sleep on the couch," she said. "You can't go out in this storm."

No way was I going to be late for our trip to the mountains in the morning. I had to get home now. "It's no big deal, Allison." I gave her a kiss good night. "I know what I'm doing."

When she opened the door, reality hit me with a cold blast. Several feet had fallen over the past few hours and snow was still coming down hard. Her driveway and my car were buried under a thick carpet of white. For a split second I considered Allison's offers. Then I thought of the mountain covered in fresh powder—perfect snowboarding conditions.

I brushed off my car as best I could, waved to Allison at the window, and headed down the drive. The wind blew viciously, and drifting snow was overtaking the road. I tried to concentrate on the fact that tomorrow's snowboarding would be worth this slick ride home. But to be honest, I was scared. I did something I had never done behind the wheel. I asked the Lord to be with me. "Keep me focused," I prayed as I turned onto the highway.

Huge powdery snowdrifts swept across the icy strip of road, and each gust of wind blew more snow into my path. Snowboarding suddenly seemed like a ridiculous reason for driving through a blizzard. I had yet to pass another car. If only Curtis and Fletcher were here—one in the back seat, the other riding shotgun—we'd be laughing and telling stories.

The farther I drove, the harder the snow came down. It was impossible to drive faster than twenty-five miles per hour; and even at that speed, it took all my attention to guide my car through the snow. I could only see about ten feet ahead of me; beyond that, it was pitch black. I felt alone in the world. Until I sensed something, or someone, beside me.

"Don't lose it now, Matt," I told myself. "You are alone out here." But I couldn't ignore the "presence." It grew until it filled my entire car. I glanced at the passenger seat and in the back, but I saw no one.

An indescribable warmth came over me. Then a feeling of intense excitement. I wasn't caught in that blizzard alone; someone was beside me. I felt completely safe. A few unexpected tears rolled down my cheeks. "Thank you, Lord!" I shouted.

Shortly thereafter, the presence left my car. But it stayed within me and I knew it would get me home.

In the distance, something luminous appeared. It got brighter, as if it were a beacon, and I headed directly for it.

Coming closer I saw a floodlight in the yard of a church. I drove past it, only to meet up with the taillights of a county snowplow. The truck made a path through the snow and threw down gravel on the road ahead of me. I turned onto my street almost seven miles later.

When I finally pulled into my driveway, I was still feeling the excitement of having that presence fill my car. Wouldn't my mom be surprised to hear that even nowadays the one "riding shotgun" can be a great protector!

A Sunny Day

Jennifer Baird

om, you said I could go to the movies today," I whined. "You always ask me to baby-sit at the last minute. You really need to tell me these things before I make other plans."

Mom did not answer as she shut the door, and I was left alone on another Saturday afternoon with my five-year-old sister and a silent, boring house. Determined to have a good day, I grabbed an old blanket, my books, and a glass of ice water and hurried to the sun in the front yard. A perfect, cool breeze billowed the blanket in mothball-scented waves as I spread it on the grass. I brought Katherine's crayons and paper, stamps and coloring books, glue and glitter until she was buried under paper like a father buried under sand at the beach. This was my refuge from baby-sitting. I wanted to study for my biology final in peace while Katherine entertained herself.

The sun, the white puffy clouds, and the sounds of neighborhood kids on bicycles and roller skates forced me to realize that my biology vocabulary was swimming in my mind. I couldn't tell a chloroplast from a crocodile. Katherine seemed content. She was drawing a green-and-purple portrait of my basset hound, Chelsea. I shut my binder and textbook and joined Katherine on the blanket. I pushed her books and boxes of markers aside to give myself room.

Katherine's freckles were like miniature stones on a tan beach. Her brown hair had escaped the usual work of Mom's brush and lay disheveled about her shoulders. The sky stretched out in limitless blue. Suddenly feeling carefree and experimental, I asked the child artist at my side, "What does God look like?"

She moved her head slightly to the side, thinking, as her tiny fingers dragged a brick-red crayon across the page. "He has a big yellow belly like a fuzzy bear's," she said, "and he has purple eyes that are kind and gentle like Bambi's."

"And where is he?" I asked.

Undistracted from her masterpiece, she answered, "Every-where." The light voice was like a soft morning rain on the surface of a lake.

"I've been told he lives in heaven."

"Yes, he's there, too—you're on my brown crayon."

I reached under my back and released the captive color. "Where else is he?" I asked. "Can you see him in other people?"

She tossed her hair out of her face and seemed a little confused about why I had so many questions. Five-year-olds are not often appreciated for their opinions. "Yes, I see him in people when they smile."

"Do you see him in me?"

Casually, she said, "Yes."

The neighbor's cat, Beasley, was stalking prey on a tree branch above our heads. A small squirrel stood quivering at the end of the branch. The breeze suddenly flapped leaves in Beasley's face, and the squirrel escaped. "What happens to people when they die?" I asked.

"They go to live with God."

"Where?"

"Up there, I think."

Down from the tree, Beasley sauntered up to my hand and made an obvious bid to be scratched.

"Have you talked to God?"

"Oh, yes. He likes to talk with me."

"Have you met him?"

"Yes."

"When?"

"A long time ago."

I considered all the books written about improving or even starting a relationship with God, and the numbers of people who go to church every Sunday, the people who think they can work hard to understand or believe in God, as if he were some math problem. A child had shown me that true knowledge of God's presence and his involvement in one's life does not come from church, effort, or age. It does not require Bible study. Katherine sees and knows God because she is not blind to what is inside of her.

The backyard of our house extends to the access road of a major freeway, and the noise of speeding cars and ambulances creeps into our daily lives. News on our radios and TVs bring information of murders and lies and debt. But in the midst of this sits a little girl—crowned with light brown hair and with her face kissed by freckles—a tiny package of faith.

This child will probably never know it, but that afternoon she reminded me of some things that I had let die inside of me. Fortunately these things are like an eternal flower that never actually dies but only fades until we let the sunlight in so they can bloom.

My Brother Cubby

Adam DePrince

In late 1985 I was given the choice to allow another brother to enter my life. Cubby entered bringing trust, humor, and love. Now, five years later, I am being given no choice about his leaving. Cubby has AIDS.

During the week of Christmas 1985, my parents were asked by the New Jersey Division of Youth and Family Services to consider the adoption of two preschoolers with hemophilia. One administrator said, "You already have so many hemophiliacs, why not two more?"

My mom, my younger brother, Erik, and I had all been born with a rare bleeding disorder, the control of which required transfusions of a frozen, concentrated blood product. In 1980 we had adopted Mikey, a baby with a severe case of classic hemophilia. He required frequent infusions of a different blood product. Intravenous equipment and syringes were as common around our house as forks and spoons in any ordinary household. What difference would two more beds and a few more cases of clotting factor make?

To be fair to the entire family, my parents felt that we should all be in agreement about the adoptions. I had always enjoyed my role as a big brother. I looked forward to the coming of our new family members, Cubby and Teddy.

I have chosen to tell the story of Cubby, my youngest brother, whose real name is Charles, because it is through him that I have learned to place my trust in God.

Cubby is truly a funny child. He is just naturally that way. He is also naturally loving and trusting. It is my funny and poignant experiences with Cubby that I store away in my memory.

A couple of days after he was placed with us, I asked four-year-old Cubby to get dressed so that he could help me shovel the snow off the driveway. Proud that a teenager had asked for his help, he scurried off to get changed.

He came downstairs dressed in a T-shirt and shorts, convinced that shorts were proper attire for the weather. He was bewildered when I explained that it was cold outside. He insisted that it was warm. I scooped him up in my arms and carried him to the front steps in order to end his confusion. It was plain to see by the astonished look on his face that Cubby had not experienced central heating in his early years.

The following summer, while on a backpacking trip, Cubby was concerned about the fact that I had to carry so much more than he. Without warning he decided to help me carry my seventy-pound pack down a trail. I had stopped for a drink from my canteen when Cubby caught hold of the frame of my pack and proudly headed down the slope. The pack weighed thirty pounds more than Cubby, so it dragged him down the path and nearly over a cliff as I frantically chased after him.

Last fall I went for a walk with Cubby and our dog, Stripe. Because of the incline of the hill near our home, I had to help Cubby along by pushing his scooter from behind. As I was struggling with the scooter, I began to feel bad that I had not noticed before that its wheels were very tight. Cubby wears a full leg brace due to the ravages of hemorrhages in his knee joint. I wondered how he was able to ride the scooter around. At the top of the long, exhausting hill Cubby turned to me and said, "Adam, I was afraid that you might let the scooter roll backward, so I held the brake all the way up to help you."

Now that Cubby's condition is worsening, death is an issue he must confront. He knows that he has AIDS. To avoid the topic would be cruel. He has told me that he is glad that we told him the truth. Now he has time to plan what he wants to do with his very short life. He is also pleased that he can prepare to face death without being in a panic on his deathbed.

Death is impossible to deal with if there is no God. Without God, death is not only terrifying for the person dying, but it also creates an unfillable void in the lives of those left behind.

While I was on a walk with Cubby one day, he was asking me questions about heaven. I was deeply touched that this nine-year-old would put so much trust in me. As much as I preferred not to discuss death, I knew I could not let my brother down. I explained to him that life does not end with death. Passing on to heaven is another, and better, part of life. If we are not afraid of being born, then we should not be afraid of dying. I told Cubby that in heaven there is no suffering and that we live with God.

Cubby was comforted to know that there are no crippled legs or hemophilia or AIDS in heaven. But he was still concerned about missing his family. I reminded him that if there were no suffering, then there could be no homesickness.

At eighteen, I'm not much of a theologian or a child psychiatrist, so I must admit that I agreed with my brother that pizza and the Teenage Mutant Ninja Turtles would surely be found in heaven. I also promised him that his permanently straight leg would bend in heaven, thus enabling him to fulfill his dream of riding a bicycle.

Cubby was worried that there would be a wait to get into heaven, such as there is at Disney World in December. I assured him that for him there would never be a line for heaven.

Falling Leaves

Rose Weill

I'm falling. . . . time slows as the rubber sole of my shoe slips from its precarious hold on the rock. My fingers claw for something to grasp—a crack, a small ledge—but I cannot overcome gravity's relentless pull. The solid rock wall rushes into a blur before my eyes.

Suddenly, the gray surface comes into focus again. I hang suspended eight feet off the ground, caught by the harness wrapped securely around my waist.

"I've got you, Rose."

Her hands fastened tightly around the rope, Bianca, my belayer, gives me a reassuring smile. Relieved, I grin back down at her and at the four other high schoolers in our outdoor adventure club. On this warm fall afternoon, we are in Great Falls, Virginia. Here upon the jagged cliffs that rise above the Potomac River, my friends and I face our challenge: to learn to rock climb.

Brushing a dry leaf out of my hair, I turn back to face the cold, unforgiving mass I must conquer. I perch my shoe upon a piece of quartz, doubtful that the tiny foothold will support me. To compensate for the lack of balance in my feet, my arm moves about my head in a clock-like motion, searching for a safe handhold. No matter where I place my hands, I am greeted by the possibility of another fall. Frustrated, I arch my neck and squint up at the towering rock face. Its height is daunting.

With my shoulders and forearms aching from tension, my fingers clutch fiercely at the cliff. After a few exhausting pulls, I manage to make some progress. I look around, scanning this new portion of the rock face. To my right, a tiny foothold catches my eye, but I quickly dismiss it; I could never balance myself on such a small crack. Unfortunately, I have no other options. Paralyzed by uncertainty, I cling to the rock. Fatigue creeps into my arms and legs. My breathing becomes heavier. Under the strain my knees begin to tremble. I realize that soon my tense muscles will give out, exhausted. A flash of fear strikes the pit of my stomach. What if I can't make it?

"Push up with your legs, Rose," someone encourages from below. I remain pinned in place. I'll be safe as long as I don't move.

I bite my lip. My energy drains with each passing moment. I let out a sigh of hopelessness. Yet as I exhale, my body relaxes a bit. A soft breeze blows, and I hear the rustling of autumn leaves. Taking a breath, I close my eyes and pray. "In thee, O Lord, do I put my trust." Slowly, my hands start to slide. The perspiration on my palms eliminates any friction that might slow me. "For thou art my rock and my fortress." The skin beneath my nails turns white as I strengthen my grip. "Therefore, for thy name's sake, lead me and guide me."

I open my eyes and peer up at the sky. I fall under the spell of one of the most enchanting sights on earth: falling leaves.

Framed by a pale blue sky, the brown stars come tumbling down. Mesmerized, I watch the leaves descend, only to be swept up by the breeze and carried gently from side to side. I crane my neck to follow the meandering paths of each twirling, gliding leaf. Eventually, the last silhouette floats past my face, and I am left alone with an empty sky. Strangely, I feel a tinge of sorrow for the poor leaves—once green, resilient, and full of life, and now dry and stiff with no choice save to fall to earth.

Once more I find myself staring at the rock face. My legs still tremble; my arms stay locked in position. I slowly force my body to relax. I lean back slightly, transferring my weight from muscle to bone. A tide of tension soon washes out from my arms. My knees stop their quivering dance. I glance warily at the tiny foothold I had previously rejected. "Trust in God," I tell myself.

I edge my right foot onto the tiny crack and in one smooth motion shift my weight to my right leg and push. Miraculously, the rubber bottoms of my shoes stick and I begin to rise. My hands reach upward, feeling their way up the rock. The strenuous clinging and pulling that I've been doing is not necessary; my legs do most of the work.

I feel balanced and at ease as I press into the rock and shove myself forward again. Higher and higher I climb, propelled by the muscles in my legs. The rock is no longer an enemy that I must fight and conquer. Instead, I choose to yield, bending and conforming my movements to the solid, unmoving features of its surface. The strain and resistance I felt earlier vanish, leaving in their wake exhilaration.

With relative ease I finish the climb. Holding on with one arm, I glance over my shoulder at the magnificent view. Far below, the river rushes onward. The faint thunder of distant rapids drones in my ears. Across the water, I see towering rocky cliffs. At their summit, the forest rises up, erupting in red, orange and golden branches. A light fog blends the trees and the sky, forming a soft line of undulating colors. Unwilling to disturb the tranquil scene, I remain motionless, whispering a silent thank-you to the unseen hand that helped lift me to this beautiful place.

Bianca signals that she is ready for me to rappel. I hesitate, remembering that to lower myself down, I have to relinquish contact with the rock.

"In thee, O Lord, do I put my trust."

I let go.

My Summer Place

Carey Olson

very summer, my family spends a hefty chunk of time near a carp-infested puddle in the far northeastern corner of South Dakota. The "puddle" is actually considered an extension of a larger body of water called Buffalo Lake. The two are connected by a small channel, wide enough to maneuver light boats through. The water in our portion of the lake is a thick, rich green—not something you'd want to swim in, but nice to look at, especially at sunset. The water in the big lake is more attractive for recreation. It's deeper with less algae and vast enough for speedboats, but the sunset doesn't hit it like it does ours.

The road leads south from Fargo onto Highway 10, then almost immediately swoops through the tiny town of Sisseton. A few miles past the west end of town is the golf course where my grandpa has spent his Wednesdays for over forty years. Next is beautiful and haunting Sica Hollow. The word means "place of the spirits." Many Indian legends have roots in the hollow and it's no mystery why. You can almost hear the spirits as the wind graces the trees.

When you travel past Sica Hollow, you go through lovely, rolling hills. You can get bored driving through so many nearly identical hills on a still day, but the prairie wind almost always stirs the silken grasses. Sometimes, you'd swear you saw unicorns running across them —sleek and shiny among the cattle and horses. On closer inspection, it turns out to be only the wind that is flattening the grass in dainty waves.

Eventually, the two-lane country road dips down into lower, flatter land. You see more trees and the countryside is splattered with lakes. You turn onto a gravel road, Buffalo Lake Lane. Down the road, taking twists and turns through a floodwater swamp, you finally come to the lots on the lake's shore that are annually inhabited by members of my extended family.

Just off Highway 10, a few yards past Buffalo Lake Lane, sits my church. It takes about ten minutes to walk down a swampy road from our cabin to the tiny white wooden building. It's an old place—one room with peeling white paint and a small, dilapidated cemetery nearby. Services are held in the church once or twice a year when someone from a Native American family asks to be buried here. The stones mark people from different countries and faiths, and the dates on the crumbling marble go as far back as the 1820s.

The old stained-glass windows are broken and some are resealed with cardboard and duct tape. Swallows build their nests inside and fly in and out. Everything is coated with dust and the pews are warped. But the main victim of the weather is the church piano.

It was never anything fancy, but at one time it was probably in tune. It must have had a gorgeous sound when it was played every Sunday. Now, though, after being exposed to the elements and neglected for many years, every note is off. Some of the keys don't work at all. Some make the same sound as the key above or below. A few of the high notes are a whole octave off. Some are always sustained, even when you're not pressing the squeaky pedal.

But I love to play that old piano.

Since the church is never locked, I can go there to be alone. Inside, it smells calm and musty, like an old memory. The sad, shabby piano stands there, begging to be played. I sit down on the splintered bench and blow a cloud of dust off the lonesome keyboard. Then I choose what I'll play. If I haven't brought a book, I extract something from the far recesses of my memory. If I've brought some written music, I do my best to sight-read it.

I learned Beethoven's "Für Elise" on that glorious instrument. To anyone else who might be listening, the sound coming from it would be cacophonous, but no one is there. In my head, I can hear the melodies that my fingers play, and enough of the keys are close to their intended pitch to make the tune real to me.

There's something about the sound of the piano in that church. It's so deep, mysterious and unexplainable. It's one church where I always feel at home. I can find peace in it and the purest beauty. The tones of the dying piano ring through the space, filling it with life. That life fills me in a way I can't really understand, an unexplainable feeling that brings me closer to God.

When I open the heavy door and enter the solitude of the church, I feel protected. I like to think that the gentle spirits of the people in the cemetery have found the same peace that I do in that musty little structure. A part of me will always stay there. I hope that the wind that carries the swallows in and out of the broken windows will carry the minor lament of "Für Elise" to the forgotten people in the cemetery, into the dark green water of Buffalo Lake, over the silken hills where unicorns run and through the cool, ancient shadows of Sica Hollow.

Kidnapped

Arun Skaria

Forced into a van at gunpoint, I couldn't see for a few seconds as my eyes adjusted to the dim light inside the back of the van. The man jumped into the driver's seat and started the engine. We lurched forward.

Jason and I sat across from one another on the cold metal floor. Our kidnapper had the gun on the passenger seat beside him. Neither Jason nor I said a word; we were terrified. I had been so confident on the basketball court, until I spun around right into the barrel of a handgun.

We drove for almost an hour, zooming around corners and blasting through potholes. With every turn, we slid across the floor or bounced off the sides of the van. I was so scared, I started to cry. I couldn't stop myself.

"Shut up back there or I'll kill you!" our kidnapper said.

"Don't cry," Jason whispered. "We're going to be okay." We were heading farther and farther away from the basketball courts, from the park, from our neighborhood, from my school. I wondered if I would I ever see my parents again.

Then I heard Jason whisper, "Our Father, who art in heaven . . ."

The Lord's Prayer—I thought of all the times I'd said it. At church, with my parents, on a camping trip with the Boy Scouts. It was just something we said, the one prayer I knew by heart. Now, just hearing Jason, I knew how much I needed it. "Thy kingdom come. Thy will be done . . ." I joined in.

Our voices grew stronger, and as we prayed, I felt less afraid. The words gave me courage. "Give us this day our daily bread . . .

"Shut up back there!"

We got louder as we repeated the prayer again and again. "Our Father, who art in heaven . . .

"I said shut up!" the kidnapper screamed.

The van roared right through a red traffic light. "Deliver us from evil," I prayed. Never had the words felt so right. The next moment I heard a siren. Thet came closer and closer.

"Make one sound," our abductor said, "and you're dead. We slowed to a stop. In seconds, we heard footsteps beside the van.

"Sir, please step out of your vehicle." The officer was insistent.

Slowly, our kidnapper opened his door and got out of the van. As soon as he did, I found the courage to yell, "Help! Back here! Help!" Jason yelled too, "Help! Help!" We banged on the sides of the van.

There was scuffling and we could hear muffled voices.

Suddenly, the back doors of the van burst open. Two police officers reached out their hands to help us, and we walked out into the bright sunlight. I took a deep breath and shook the tension out of my shoulders and neck as we followed the officers toward their squad car. It felt so incredibly good to be free! And I couldn't forget how it happened. When we said that prayer, all my fears left me. My courage returned, and I knew we weren't alone.

"Looks like you two had quite a ride," one of the officers said. "Good thing we heard you back there!"

Jason and I smiled at each other. "Yeah," I said. "Good thing somebody else heard us, too."

There is no fear in love, so we draw near,
Thy perfect love, O Lord, has cast out fear.

As corn before the wind bends all one way,
So would we bow before Thy wind to-day.

Our several choices, Lord, we would forgo;
Breath of the living God, O great Wind, blow.

AMY CARMICHAEL

Saved by Faith

Tornado

Janet Lucas

It startred out like any other night. I was baby-sitting for the Parkers, our neighbors who lived a mile down the road. Around seven, while I was in the driveway playing basketball with four-year-old Clint and two-year-old Eric, I heard the rumble of distant thunder. When lightning flickered on the horizon, I herded the boys indoors.

To keep their minds off the approaching storm, I asked the boys if they had any new toys. Eric and Clint proudly brought out their new plastic swords that glowed with a phosphorescent light. "See," Eric said, pressing a button on the handle. The sword's color changed from pink to white to blue, then back to pink again.

We'd just begun to play when the phone rang. "Janet!" it was my mother. "I just heard on the radio that a tornado has touched down in Bedford, and its heading east, right toward us!"

I'd barely hung up when the wind hit the house like a truck. I lunged for the boys and, clutching one under each arm, raced down the hall toward the bathroom, the only room with no windows.

The lights went out and there was a rippping sound overhead as part of the roof tore away. I shoved the boys to the bathroom floor, dropped down on top of them, and pressed my feet against the door to hold it shut. Wood splintered at the base of the door. Dirt flew up through the drains of the tub and sink. The walls vibrated.

I must have been shaking too. I started to sing, "Jesus loves me, this I know, for the Bible tells me so . . ." The Bible had told me to stay calm, have courage, and trust God. I sang even louder and the boys joined in, "little ones to him belong. They are weak, but he is strong."

In the midst of this crazy storm, I was aware that we all belonged to someone bigger. I heard a final ripping sound, a crash, then silence. We lay in the darkness and Eric started to cry.

"Keep singing," I said. "I'll be back in a minute."

I groped my way through the debris, looking for some kind of light. The carpets were crusted with broken glass, but then, in the inky blackness, I saw two slivers of light: the boys' swords. Even though it looked as if all the other toys had blown away, the swords lay there, unharmed. I clutched them to my chest and scrambled back to the bathroom.

The gentle glow of the swords calmed the boys immediately, and the changing colors seemed to soothe them, like a symbol of God's presence, a small gesture that said, "Yes, I'm with you. I can use the simplest things to bring you comfort."

Neighbors arrived several minutes later, and we stumbled out of the house. Part of the roof was gone, along with every window and door. Their TV antenna curved toward the ground like a giraffe bent over to drink. Pine trees looked like blades of grass that had been trampled on by a monstrous foot.

"Weren't you scared?" people asked me. "How did you know what to do?"

At first I wondered the same thing. Yes, I was scared, and I expect that someday I'll be scared again. But now I know something I didn't know before the night of the tornado. When I am in a crisis and others are relying on me, if I rely on God, he will give me the strength I need. And that is real "responsibility."

Clancy

Lori Hasenyager

No doubt about it: I'm an animal lover. Maybe that's because I grew up on a farm, surrounded by lots of animals. To me, horses and dogs and cats aren't just pets—they're family. And there's no dog in the world like my black lab Clancy.

I got Clancy one sunny spring day, when I happened to walk by a house near our farm at the bottom of Mount Spokane, Washington. Outside was a sign advertising a free black lab. I had graduated from college that year, and I felt like a new dog was just what I needed to keep me company. So I knocked on the door.

"Our kids are all grown and gone," the owner explained. "Clancy needs more attention than my wife and I can give him."

The man showed me the backyard where the dog was sitting inside a small fenced in area. Looking up at me with sad eyes, he wagged his tail on the hard ground. I melted. "Okay, I'll take him!"

Clancy and I hit it off right away. Every morning and evening I'd go out to feed the horses, and Clancy would be right at my heels. He'd run ahead, then charge back as fast as he could for a quick pat or playful bop on the head, only to turn and race ahead again. After chores, we'd walk down to the stream that ran behind our pasture. Clancy loved to swim. He'd jump right in, dog paddling back and forth like a pro until I'd call him and tell him it was time to go. Then he'd climb out and give himself a good shake before we headed back to the house.

By February, Clancy and I were old pals, and we never missed our playtime after feeding the horses. So one afternoon after I finished chores, I wasn't surprised when Clancy headed off down the road that ran past our house. The sun was beginning to set and there was a chill in the air, so I was glad I'd worn my coat and boots to trudge through the wet snow. Oh Clancy, I thought, it's too cold for your swim. Plus, with all the early runoff from the mountain, our little creek had risen. It looked more like a river than a small stream. I guess Clancy didn't mind the cold or the extra water. I knew right where he was headed. He had discovered a new spot, where the creek flowed under a bridge in the nearby road. There, the water formed a small pool, and he could swim in place against the current. It was hilarious to watch. Clancy had his own private whirlpool.

But as we followed the road to the bridge that afternoon, I noticed the level of water had risen really high. The barbed-wire fence that ran alongside the bridge and across the creek was now engulfed by a torrent of rushing water.

Before I could stop him, Clancy jumped off the bridge. Worried, I looked over the wooden railing. There was Clancy, paddling hard in the whirlpool. This current's a lot more than he's used to, I thought. I whistled and called, "Clancy! Come on out, boy! Come on!"

Clancy turned his head toward me, but he obviously couldn't come. He was struggling to stay afloat in the fast waters; and he was getting pushed closer and closer to the barbed-wire fence, where it crossed the creek.

"Clancy! Come, boy! You can do it! Now!"

My heart broke as he sputtered and fell slowly beneath the dark water. I stood, frozen in place trying to reassure myself. "Just watch; he'll come up on the other side of the fence and swim to the bank," I thought. Seconds passed and no Clancy. Then I knew that he must be tangled in the barbed wire beneath the surface.

I ran down the embankment by the fence, close to where Clancy had disappeared. Grabbing the wire fence with one gloved hand, I stepped into the rushing water. A split second later, the current slammed me into the barbed wire, in water up to my waist. The shocking cold took my breath away, and I felt my boots sink slowly into the muddy bottom. I stretched my free hand, reaching into the dark water where I last saw Clancy. "Lord, where is my dog?" I prayed.

I moved out farther, careful not to lose my footing. After a few steps, the embankment eroded away and I suddenly dropped deep, the water now up to my chin I held firm onto the fence with my outstretched arm, my other hand searching deep under the icy water. What was that? I felt a collar. I curled my fingers around it and pulled with all the strength I could muster.

Clancy rose to the surface, coughing and sputtering. I held him firmly by the collar under his chin, his face resting just above the surface. As soon as he saw me, he stopped struggling and relaxed in my grip.

I tried to swim toward the embankment. But my boots were stuck in the mud and the current had pinned me against the fence. I could feel the sharp points of the barbed wire as it tore my clothes and skin. I clung to the fence for support, and strained to hold Clancy with my other arm. I quickly looked around. Don't panic; just figure out how to get out of this. The late afternoon sun had fallen behind the trees and left us in a spooky glow. We were hidden behind the bridge on a road rarely traveled. I looked at Clancy. He stared back at me, with those trusting eyes reflecting the lingering last glow of the sun.

With the frigid water zapping my strength, it was all I could do just to keep both our heads up. I knew I would have to make a decision: either let go of Clancy, or hold on and risk both of us drowning. "I can't let go of Clancy, God," I prayed. "But I can't hold on much longer. Please, I need your help."

I looked up toward the road and thought I saw headlights. I didn't have enouh energy left to yell, but I could keep praying. "God, I don't know how you are going to do it. No one can possibly see us here below the bridge. But I trust you completely."

The lights neared and then crossed the bridge. It was a truck. "Please don't go," I whispered, as I struggled to keep Clancy, and myself, above the murky water. But the truck passed. "Dear God, please help us."

Suddenly, the truck stopped. It backed up and pulled to the side of the road. "Hey, hold on there!" a man shouted. We'll be right down." In seconds, two men had run down the embankment. One grabbed the fence and stretched out his hand. A new strength surged through me and I swung Clancy over so the man could reach him. He grabbed him and passed him to his buddy farther up the bank. Then he reached out again, this time for me. I was able to give him a free hand, and he pulled me out of the water, boots and all.

On the ride back to the house I asked my rescuer, "How did you ever see us in the water?"

"I really don't know," he said. "We just decided to take this road for a change. As we were talking, I happened to glance out my window and saw a flicker from the stream. I was just curious and decided to see what it was. Pretty lucky for you!"

Of course I knew it wasn't "luck" that those two guys just happened by and saw us. I'll never forget how helpless Clancy looked in the water, and how much he depended on me to get him out. And as much as I love Clancy, I know God loves me that much—and more. That's why I'll always place my trust in him.

Rescued by Light

Courtney Lee Stubbert

It had been a long day and I was glad to be on my way home, driving along a rural two-lane highway. It was the summer between my junior and senior years of high school, and a dozen or so friends from church had spent the day at my house helping me put together an above-ground swimming pool.

Late in the afternoon, we had a barbecue and agreed to meet again the next morning to finish the job. After everybody left, I drove my friend Jennifer home to Cottage Grove, about twenty miles away. We watched TV until about eleven-thirty, when I began to nod off. I was really beat, so I headed back home.

I stifled a yawn as the headlights of my 1972 Duster cut through the darkness. I felt my eyelids getting heavy. "You're almost there," I told myself. I opened the window slightly to let in some fresh air as I hummed a tune. But my eyelids grew heavier, my fingers loosened their grip on the steering wheel, and I drifted off to sleep.

The car veered off the road and onto the bumpy gravel shoulder and I came awake fast. I was speeding toward the corner of a concrete bridge. Terror shot through me, and I squeezed my eyes shut as my right headlight and front wheel smashed into the concrete.

A tremendous jolt knocked the breath out of me. The car

114

flipped over and slid to a sickening halt. I was hanging upside down from my seat belt. There was glass in my mouth and down the front of my shirt. I thought about my family and what they would do without me; how I would never go to college, never have children. A tremendous sense of loss overwhelmed me. Then I knew that I had to get out of here.

I opened my eyes and blinked away glass. I could see a few twinkling pinpoints of light from farmhouses about half a mile away. Get out, an inner voice urged. I groped for the seatbelt buckle. I closed my eyes again and slipped out of the shoulder harness. Hurry!

I crawled across the ceiling of the car, glass crunching under my hands and knees. I don't remember squeezing through the passenger-side window frame; it was as though I floated outside the car. An instant later I found myself in the middle of the road.

Rising from my hands and knees, I opened my eyes. It was no longer dark and I was swathed in a brilliant light. Squinting down, I saw the tiniest details of the asphalt; I noticed a cut across the knuckles of my right hand. I stopped under a big street lamp, and shut my eyes from the blinding light. But when I looked again, it was pitch black. Where had the light come from? I looked around but could find no possible source.

I stared up at the stars and thanked God for rescuing me. Once again I felt the irresistible urge to move. I began to run, but after about fifty paces I slowed a bit, then stopped. I turned to look back at the car. The blazing, resplendent light had vanished. It had stayed only long enough to help me. Now I was barely able to make out the car's twisted outline.

The car began to burn, and in seconds it was completely engulfed in a blazing fire. I turned away from the heat and began moving toward the nearest farmhouse, all the while thanking God for saving my life and for sending me light when all was darkness.

Lost on the Ice

William N. Lindemann

lat on my face in frozen snow, gasping for breath, I knew that if I didn't get back on my feet I would surely die. I struggled to my knees and shakily rose—only to be slammed down again by a blast of icy snow. Was the howling Wisconsin blizzard going to kill me?

Two hours earlier, under an overcast sky on that cold January day in 1975, I started hiking across the twenty-five miles of Lake Mendota in Madison, Wisconsin. The frigid air pinched my nostrils but I loved it. When I grew up in Wisconsin, I had always explored the outdoors—paddling, climbing, wandering the woods. I respected nature but did not fear it.

In my childhood I believed it was because Mother assured me that my guardian angel would watch over me. But by my teen years I no longer believed in such fairy-tale stuff. Rebellious and headstrong, I ran away from home. I had convinced myself that I was a man totally in control.

At age nineteen I moved to Madison and enrolled in the University of Wisconsin. On that particular afternoon I decided to skip class and walk across the frozen lake near my apartment house. I bundled up for my trek in a hooded down parka, heavy logging boots, and insulated leather mittens.

The big lake had been frozen for many weeks and the ice was quite thick, except around the breakwater. As I stood onshore, I could see people ice fishing in the distance. I figured it would take about two hours to reach the lake's center, where I would decide whether to continue on to the other side or return home. I created a line-of-sight target and stomped off into the snow.

It was a tiring walk and, because I was thirsty, I started eating snow. When I reached the lake's center, the wind had picked up and the temperature had plummeted. Ominous clouds formed overhead. Snowflakes whirled around me and I could no longer see anyone on the ice. Soon I was swallowed in a blizzard and had to shield my eyes from the stinging crystals. I wanted to turn back toward campus but I had lost my bearings.

The gale rose in crescendo. I was snow-blind, engulfed by the whiteout. The driving blizzard took my breath away. Drawing my hood more tightly around my face, I staggered on, looking down and desperately trying to see my boots and keep walking toward land in a straight line.

Stumbling upon a drift, I fell flat on my face. I tried to rise but I was so disoriented I fell again. There was nothing to do but crawl. Against the ferocious wind, I began working my way across the snow, stretching one hand out as far as possible, digging it in, pulling my knee up to it and arching my back in a kind of inch-worm fashion. Every so often thunderous groans rolled up through the slowly shifting ice.

Despair drained any self-confidence I had left and a sense of doom filled me. I did not know in which direction I was going. I sank my forehead against the ice, finally admitting I was totally helpless. At that moment, I knew if I didn't get back on my feet I would die. "God, if you're out there and want me to live," I cried, "you're going to have to do something!"

Suddenly, above the howling wind I heard a deep warning sound like a foghorn. I looked around, but I couldn't tell where it was coming from. I called out, "Make it loud and clear."

Ooooooommm. This time I oriented myself to the direction of the sound. I realized it had come from the rescue station which was only blocks from my apartment. As I crawled toward it I heard a voice: "Be careful. Watch out for the breakwater. The water is open and deep."

I remembered the breakwater near the rescue station and knew that if I fell in I would die in seconds. I felt ahead with my hand and dragged myself across bumpy snow and ice. After awhile I heard water lapping. Again the voice guided me: "Stay to the right; climb the concrete wall when you reach it."

Soon the waves sounded close and when I pulled my gloved hand to my face, it was wet. After sliding on my belly to the right, I caught a faint yellow light from the rescue station. The light gave me renewed strength. I worked my way onto the bank and struggled through deep snow to the station and banged on the door with my frozen glove.

The door was pulled open immediately and strong arms reached out and half-carried me inside. The room was snug and warm. As I blinked away frozen snow, my eyes made out a tall, dark-haired man looking at me. He asked if I was all right.

He said he had spotted me out on the lake and had set the warning horn off thinking it might guide me. He asked if I wanted some coffee.

I nodded gratefully and took the cup he offered, wrapped my icy hands around it, and savored the warmth. I asked him why he was working there in midwinter, and he said he was finishing some research. After I finished the coffee and felt revived, but still too dazed to ask my rescuer's name, I thanked him profusely, walked out the door, and made it home.

At the apartment my roommates were curious. I had been gone over seven hours. When I told them what had happened, one wrinkled his brow. "There's no way that rescue station would be open this time of year," he said.

With the taste of the coffee still in my mouth, I replied groggily, "Just a coincidence, I guess." Then I went to bed for a long, deep sleep.

The next morning the storm had passed and I walked back to the rescue station to find out more about my mysterious benefactor and to thank him properly. The entrance was nearly buried in snow. After I worked my way to the door, I found a sign affixed to it: CLOSED FOR WINTER. I peered inside through a window and could see that the place was empty.

I couldn't believe it. Someone had been there the previous night. A man had talked to me and served me coffee.

I called the university and was told that the Safety Department ran the rescue station. The Safety Department said that the station was closed for the season. As a last resort, I called the Dane County Sheriff's office; they couldn't help me either.

But all the while, growing suspicion told me my search would prove fruitless. For I soon understood who that man in the rescue station was. My mother had told me about him long ago. Everyone entrusted with a mission is an angel.

Never Too Late

Stuart Reininger

When I was a troubled teen growing up in New York City, I had a secret refuge I escaped to—the rooftop of the tenement building where my family lived on Shakespeare Avenue in the Bronx. I could gaze across the Harlem River all the way downtown to the soaring spires of Manhattan—a shimmering lure to a better life. Divorce and alcoholism had rocked my family; poverty ground us down. But up there, gazing at the skyline, I vowed that someday I was going to be somebody, no matter what it took.

At fifteen, I was already amassing credentials as a delinquent: I had been arrested for car theft and thrown out of one school. I landed at Haaren High in the Hell's Kitchen section of Manhattan. More than anything, I wanted to be respected by the tough gang members who stalked the halls of my high school. But then a boy named Billy changed my life.

Haaren, an all-boys school, was a looming, fortresslike gray stone building on West Fifty-ninth Street. Most of us were just marking time until we turned seventeen and could drop out without a hassle. The halls were dingy and the stairwells covered with gang graffiti. You knew which gang a kid belonged to by the colors he wore or the insignia on his leather jacket. Everyone belonged to some group.

Except me. I never seemed to fit in. I was the best car thief in school, but that didn't count. To be really tough you had to show that you were willing to do practically anything. Even though I was small for my age, I talked tough and looked tough in the armor of my leather jacket, my ducktail haircut, and pegged jeans. But others saw through it. When the dismissal bell rang at 3:00 P.M. and a rampaging horde of my peers erupted onto Tenth Avenue, shoving pedestrians, snapping the antennae off parked cars, and slashing tires just for the malicious fun of it, I hung back. The violence bothered me. I tried to duck the "blanket parties," where a gang would surround a kid, throw a blanket over him and beat him up. Stealing cars was different. It was impersonal and done in the dark of night. I never had to face the owners whose property I had swiped and damaged.

One night during my junior year I staked out a beautiful new T-bird and invited another boy to go for a joyride with me. But when the time came to hot-wire the car, I couldn't get it started. Frantically I worked under the dashboard. Just then a police cruiser turned the corner and I lost my cool. I fled in a panic, barely making an escape. I felt like a fool.

Word got around Haaren fast. A few afternoons later while I was walking down a stairwell between classes, someone threw a blanket over me, and I was beaten to a pulp.

Riding the subway home to the Bronx, the shame of the beating pained me far more than the bruises that covered my body. The subway car was filled with people who seemed to have some purpose in life: the guy in a suit and tie reading the paper on his way home from work; a young couple with their baby; an older woman studying the Bible. What did I have? I wasn't even acceptable to a bunch of hoods!

That night, when I got to my building, I ran all the way up the stairs to the roof. Sweaty and breathless, I collapsed in the cool night air. Over the roar of the nearby elevated trains I screamed out my frustration to the skyline in the near distance.

A few weeks later Billy Blankenship was murdered. I didn't know him. He was my age and lived a few blocks from me. Billy came from a close-knit family and was an honor student at a good school. Everyone said he had a bright future. Except Billy was in the wrong place at the wrong time. In a dreadful case of mistaken identity, he was gunned down by a gang member who thought Billy belonged to a rival outfit. The shooter was from Haaren.

The tabloids went crazy with the story. They ran pictures of the Blankenship family and interviews with the parents. I couldn't relate to Billy, but I discovered I had a lot in common with the seventeen-year-old murderer. I also came from a poor family. I often slept on the subways when I didn't want to go back to our tenement flat. I didn't carry a gun, but wouldn't have minded if people thought I did.

The students at Haaren basked in the notoriety. I wore my school jacket and swaggered down the street bragging, "You know, the school that guy who shot the Blankenship kid went to. Yeah, I hung out with him." It made me feel like somebody.

One day after class I was with a bunch of my schoolmates in the basement of an abandoned building near Haaren. I was regaling them with my latest car-theft exploit when suddenly one of the older boys grabbed my arm, dragged me to the center of the group and whipped a gun out of his pocket.

"Would you know what to do with this?" he snarled, jamming the gun under my nose. I stared at the small nickel-plated automatic. My mouth went dry and I broke into a sweat.

"Nah, you wouldn't be able to do nothin'. You'd be shakin' too much, just like you are now!"

Everyone started laughing. The boy with the gun slapped me hard on the back of the head and shoved me toward the door. I wiped away hot tears of shame as the jeers chased me up the steps.

When I got home, I ran to the rooftop, curled up in a corner, and cried my eyes out. Everything that had ever gone wrong in my life seemed to come back to humiliate me all at once.

"God," I sobbed, "why won't they accept me? I don't want to shoot anybody. I just want to belong." Maybe it wasn't right to ask God to help me get into a gang, but I just didn't know what else to do. I felt profoundly lost and alone.

Later that night in the cramped bedroom I shared with my younger brother, I snatched a newspaper off the floor. There was a story about Billy Blankenship's funeral. The writer told about how the family's faith was guiding them through the tragedy of Billy's death.

Against my will, the story moved me. I read what people said about Billy. "Billy loved to read." I love to read, I thought. "Billy had a curiosity about everything. He loved science." So do I, but nobody ever told me that was a good thing. "Billy had a deep faith in God." I believe in God, too, but I'm usually ashamed to admit it. With a flash of guilt I wondered what people would say about me. Billy was a good kid; and strangely enough, there were a lot of qualities he and I shared. We had both hoped for great futures, but now his was over and mine was quickly disappearing. Then it struck me like a thunderbolt: Billy would not have been accepted by any of the gangs at my school. He never would have wanted to be.

All of a sudden, neither did I. I paced all night, startled by my newfound revelation. I didn't belong with those people. I didn't have to join a gang to overcome the fear and frustration in my life. I had qualities that I wanted people to remember when they talked about me. That night, as I paced and thought and prayed, something assured me that I belonged to God, that he listened and cared, and all he wanted was for me to live my life well.

As the sun rose, I climbed the stairs to the roof again and looked out over the city through the hazy dawn. Billy's life had ended, but mine was just beginning. I wanted to make the most of it.

Shark!

Mike Coots

Born to board. That's me. By the time I could walk, I could swim in the ocean. Mom got me a bodyboard—a short surfboard that you lie on instead of standing—when I was five and took me to a beach where the surf was safe for a kid. I paddled out, ready for action. I kept slipping off the board. Finally I caught a wave. It was just a little, kid-sized wave; but riding it, I felt like I was going a million miles an hour all the way to shore.

After that, I lived to go boarding. Before school, after school—whether the waves were big or small, I was out there riding them. I joined a bodyboarding team and won a junior national championship in my sophomore year of high school. The year I graduated, I was seriously thinking about going pro. In fact, I'd been praying about it, totally trusting that God would lead me.

The morning of October 28, my boarding buddy, Kyle Maligro, our coach, Bob Sato, and I got up around five o'clock to hit the surf at Majors Bay, a secluded spot on the west side of Kauai. Early morning is the best time to be in the water. There's usually no wind so the surface is smooth and glassy, and there aren't too many people around. Only about eight other guys were with us in the water that day as we drifted about 150 yards offshore. Bob was on the beach with a video camera.

I looked around. The water was murky. That's a problem. In bad visibility, sharks can sometimes mistake a dude on a board for a sea turtle. A couple of attacks get written up in the papers each year. Tiger sharks—a big, aggressive species that's pretty common around here—are often responsible. But I figured just about every sport has its dangers. I could take care of myself.

Kyle hopped a big wave and rode it to shore. Lying on my three-foot board with my legs dangling in the water, I glanced over my shoulder. The first in the next set of big waves was coming in. The trick in bodyboarding is to be at just the right spot when a wave breaks. Catch it too far out, and it'll move past without you. Catch it too far in, and you'll get tumbled underwater. I looked back to check out the wave better. There was a sudden pressure on my right leg—like something really big was pushing against me.

My hand touched something rough. I turned and saw the broad gray head of a tiger shark. It had its massive jaws clamped on me like a dog on a bone. It dumped me off my board and shook its head back and forth, its teeth sawing through the flesh of my legs, while I tried to grab the safety leash.

It was weird, but I didn't feel any pain right then. Everything was happening in a blur, like a dream. I had to get my legs out. Without thinking, I jammed my arm into the shark's mouth and tried to yank myself free. Nothing doing. I pulled my arm out. Blood streamed from it. The shark wasn't letting go. "I'm not going down without a fight!" I thought. I clenched my fist, drew it over my head, then brought it down on that shark's snout. *Thwamp!*

With a thrash of its tail, the huge animal released its grip and sank out of sight. I jerked my board back to me by the leash. The big wave I'd been watching was almost on top of me. "Please, God," I prayed, "let me catch this wave before that shark comes back.

I paddled like crazy. The wave swept me up, and I ripped

down its face. I felt my right leg begin to spasm. "Man, how bad did it get me?" I turned around. My leg ended at mid-calf. The sight was so surreal, it didn't really register. All I knew was that I needed to keep riding that wave. It took me right into the shallows. I ditched my board and tried to get up. Immediately I collapsed.

"Hang on, dude. I've got you." Kyle slung his arm around my shoulder and helped me hop up onto the beach. He grabbed the leash off my bodyboard and tied it super-tight around my calf to staunch the blood flow.

Bob ran up. "I'm going for help," he said, then raced off. Majors Bay is off the beaten path, and our car was parked pretty far away. Even with the leash tied around my leg like a tourniquet, blood was flooding onto the sand. I'd never seen so much blood in my life.

Kyle dropped to his knees right next to me. "God," he said, "I know you're here with us. Please help save Mike."

A feeling of absolute calm swept over me. "Lord, I don't know how you're planning to get me out of this, but I trust you. Totally."

A truck tore down the beach and pulled up next to us. The driver jumped out. "My name's Keith," he said. "I just stopped to check out the waves a minute ago. I saw the whole thing."

Keith and Kyle lifted me into the back of the pickup, and we took off for Kauai Veterans Hospital in Waimea, fifteen miles of twisting, winding island roadway. Keith floored it, passing car after car. I saw the shocked expressions on the drivers' faces when they noticed me. I was getting real dizzy and chilled from all the blood I'd lost. "Maybe I'm not going to make it after all," I thought. But I wasn't scared. "God, I know you won't leave me."

By the time we pulled up at Kauai Veterans Hospital, I was on the verge of blacking out. The doctors there stopped the blood flow and stabilized me with a transfusion, then sent me on to Wilcox Hospital in Lihue, where they were better equipped to handle trauma cases.

A couple of days later, I was well enough to get in a wheelchair and join my family, friends and some of the hospital staff in a prayer circle, not to plead for my recovery but to give thanks for my survival. If I hadn't caught that big wave into shore seconds after the attack, and if Kyle hadn't immediately tied that cord around my leg to stem the bleeding, and if Keith hadn't shown up with his truck when he did, I wouldn't be here. At every moment, every second, I'd gotten exactly the help I needed.

I get around pretty well with my prosthesis, although I don't use it in the water. There's less drag with one leg, so I'm faster than ever. Reaching the pro bodyboarding ranks is definitely in sight. But more than anything, I'm really grateful: Grateful to be alive and grateful to have God in my life. The best part of still riding the waves is knowing he's out there, riding them with me.

Shipwrecked

Chris Napolitano

At nineteen, I was proud to be at sea, free of school, away from home, and independent of parents who, I felt, couldn't understand why I wanted to taste life first-hand. Now I was at the helm of the forty-foot sailing ketch *Reality*, listening to the bow plowing through the water.

Just a week before, I had stood on *Reality's* foredeck as we slipped out of the Annapolis, Maryland, harbor. I was in the middle of my sophomore year of college, but I longed for excitement. So on Christmas break I posted my name with a Port of Annapolis yacht dealer as a potential crew member. Within a few days, a dealer phoned to tell me that a man was leaving January 7 for Florida with his new ketch—a large, specially equipped sailboat.

The voyage was everything I had dreamed. I had not sailed much, so I enjoyed my four-hour watches: to feel the ketch heel before the wind as her masts swayed against a starry sky.

As we followed the Intracoastal Waterway, clouds of herons launched themselves from the surface of the water. We spent lazy days lounging on deck as we exchanged views on world affairs and the nature of God.

Now, as the morning sun tried to break through an overcast

January sky, we were about ten miles off the Florida coast and expected to make our destination in another three days.

I was chatting with Jerry Willis, skipper and owner of the fiberglass ketch, in the cockpit when Doug Dixon, the other member of our crew, burst up the companionway, and shouted, "We're flooding!"

Jerry grabbed the radio and started calling, "Mayday! Mayday!" He ordered Doug and me to get the buckets. But as icy seawater climbed up our shins, it was obvious that *Reality* would sink in a few minutes.

"Get the life raft!" Doug yelled. I scrambled to the deck and, in spite of the ship's lurching and my numb-with-cold fingers, began to loosen the straps that held the raft. Fear was rising in my throat.

Jerry still tried to raise someone on the radio as he hurled food and water to stash in the raft. Then I heard him yell, "Abandon ship!" At that instant, a surge of water rolled over the side of the boat and *Reality's* decks were underwater. Doug and I found ourselves struggling in the cold Atlantic. I watched the ketch's bow rise out of the water then disappear in a roll of foam. Doug and I swam away from the tug of the sinking ship, trying not to get caught in its wake.

Then we saw the raft burst to the surface with a sputtering Jerry right behind. He had been dragged down thirty feet by the rigging before he could free himself. We swam to the raft and pulled ourselves onto it, dazed and exhausted. All of our food and water were gone. We had only a hand compass, life jackets, one poncho, and the clothes on our backs. Jerry had a four-inch knife tucked in his belt. We didn't even have anything with which to bail water.

Someone will find us, I thought. We're only ten miles from shore. But a cold offshore wind blew us out to sea. With each swell of the waves, the cold spray drenched us and we huddled together for warmth.

Hours later Jerry shouted, "A freighter!" We stood up in the raft and waved our yellow life jackets as we futilely screamed ourselves hoarse. But the ocean swells hid us from view, and the freighter steamed out of sight. We slumped into the raft and lay down as darkness fell. Surely someone would find us in the morning.

We tried to cover ourselves with the poncho to keep warm, but we only slept fitfully. When a wave flooded the raft, we bailed the water with my tennis shoes. Even the rising sun brought no warmth as it was soon obscured by thick clouds.

By the end of the second day, I knew we suffered from dehydration. Another frigid night and the third day of gray sky and sea passed with no ships coming close enough to spot us. On the fourth morning we lay in a daze in the bottom of the raft.

Freighters passed on the horizon; but after we waved our life jackets a few times, we gave up. Our world had shrunk to a six-foot rubber tub where we lay tortured by cold, dehydration, and painful skin rashes from the saltwater. We estimated we were now ninety miles out to sea.

That night I dreamed that I had gone ashore to buy some roasted peanuts. But when I awakened, I saw only the same gray sea and black sky. Huddling back under the poncho with Doug and Jerry, I fell into a semiconscious daze in which we all now existed. I could hear someone mumbling, "Lord, if it be your will, save us, If not, don't prolong our suffering. Do away with us now,"

Suddenly a terrific blow struck the bottom of the raft, throwing me several inches in the air. Immediately, all three of us were on our knees looking at the ocean. what we saw were the black dorsal fin and tail of a shark as it cut through the water.

"Look!" gasped Doug, "he's out to get us!"

We stared in horror as the monster, at least fourteen feet long, circled our raft. Then it charged toward us like a torpedo. Jerry knelt at the edge of the raft with his small knife. As the shark surged at us, it rolled so it could tear at the raft with its teeth, I looked straight into its eye. Jerry's arm swept downward, then he was on his knees gasping for air. The knife must have penetrated the shark's tough hide, because it swam away leaving a trail of blood. "Thank God," I said.

"Look!" Jerry cried. A large oil tanker was only about half a mile away. We waved our life jackets and called hysterically. But again, no one saw us, and the tanker continued on its course. I leaned my head down on the raft and prayed, "Please, Lord Jesus in heaven, turn someone's head on that boat."

"It's coming! It's coming!" cried Doug, I looked up as the tanker's bow headed toward us.

Over an hour later, suffering from shock and dehydration and barely able to walk, we were given first aid on the tanker. I thanked the third mate and asked him how he had happened to spot us.

"I don't know really," he said, looking puzzled. "I was looking through my binoculars in the opposite direction when something told me to turn around and I saw you. If you had been lying down, we never would have seen you."

I knew who had turned his head. It was the same one who sent the shark to arouse us, the one with whom I was beginning a real adventure that would last for the rest of my life.

The Girl Nobody Wanted

Stephanie Fast

After the end of the Korean war I was conceived by the union of a Korean woman with an American soldier, probably in the city of Pusan. As a child of mixed blood, I was considered a nonperson. I was abandoned at about the age of four and began living on the streets. Many orphaned children of mixed blood were killed; others were picked off the streets and sent to America by adoption agencies. I wasn't.

I learned to snatch morsels from food stalls, to be at butcher shops when they threw out the bones, and to roast grasshoppers on rice straw. At night I'd roll myself into a straw mat and sleep under a bridge. I never dreamed of acceptance from adults; I was a half-breed—a dirty *toogee*—an ugly reminder of an ugly war. Even other street children taunted me. They'd send me to steal food and reasoned that as a nonperson, I wouldn't feel the pain of a beating if I got caught.

Once I was tied to a waterwheel and nearly drowned. Another time I was thrown down an abandoned well. I screamed for help until I had no more voice, then watched as the patch of light at the top turned to darkness. I found a stone sticking out of the wall and sat there, cold and numb. I wondered how long it would be before I was dead. Then I heard the voice of an old woman: "Little girl, are you down there?"

After she hauled me out with the well's bucket, she hurried me to a barn and covered me with straw. Kind as she was, she didn't want to be seen helping a *toogee*, for fear of what her neighbors would do to her. That's why she had waited till dark to help me. "You sleep now, little girl, but before daylight, run to the mountains. If they find you here tomorrow, they'll kill you."

At dawn I fled to a mountain cave and hid. That night, huddled alone, I peered out at the stars. "Why am I so bad," I wondered, "that people want to kill me? Why can't I be like other children, who have a mommy and daddy?"

I began going from village to village, thinking, "Maybe my mom lives in one of them and will recognize me."

One day I went to the train station and stood on the platform, waiting until a train pulled in. People began spewing out of the cars; and forgetting all caution, I scurried among them, craning my neck and peering into the women's eyes so the one who was my mother could recognize me.

Any moment now, my mind raced, a woman's face will light up and she'll say, "My little girl! At last I have found you!"

But no one stopped. Time after time women brushed me out of their paths. Instead of lighting up, their eyes narrowed. I knew what they were thinking: *toogee*. The platform emptied. Just a few American soldiers stood about. Maybe one of them is my daddy. I went to them. But none of the soldiers even saw the American in me. To them I was just like all the other little beggars who filled the streets of Pusan. One of them gave me a chocolate bar that I wolfed down.

I was about seven when a cholera epidemic swept Korea. One day I fainted in the street. When I woke up I was on a mat in a bright room filled with children. A Swedish nurse had brought me to the World Vision orphanage in Taejon. I recovered and was soon strong enough to wash diapers and help feed and care for the babies.

One day the nurse told me that an American couple was coming to adopt a baby boy. I took extra care with my boys to make them look appealing. We were out in a courtyard when they arrived—huge people with pale faces like moons. The man came over, picked up one of my boys, and lovingly stroked the baby's face. Then I watched in disbelief as tears welled up in the man's eyes. I inched closer to get a better look at this strange man. He placed the baby gently back in his basket, turned to me, and then began to caress my face. My heart thumped wildly; his touch felt so good. But I had never, ever been touched except to be beaten or kicked. Child of the streets, I slapped his hand away, spit at him, and ran.

The next day this man and his wife returned. They talked to the nurse and pointed at me. Even though I was nearly nine, I weighed only thirty pounds. I had worms, my body was covered with scars, and my hair crawled with lice. I had a lazy eye that flopped around in its socket. But David and Judy Merwin chose me.

When I entered their houses, I thought I'd come to a palace. I was overwhelmed by their kindness and love. Patiently, painstakingly, they taught me English and helped me with my lessons at the American school. After awhile they took me back to America and provided me with the best home life and the best education; they gave me their all. I was living in a fairyland, and yet I was not a part of it. Deep down I still felt like a *toogee*.

I learned early that Americans like it when you smile, so I did a lot of smiling. As a young teen in Rockport, Indiana, I made many friends. Everyone loved the pleasant Korean girl who sang in the choir, taught Sunday school, and got academic awards. I smiled to please everyone because I never wanted to go back to street life again. But deep down the gnawing fear always lurked: If they only knew who I really am they would hate me.

My mother and father were disappointed when I insisted on bleaching my hair and buying deep-blue contact lenses so I could look more American. My orange hair looked strange and I lived in a dark-blue world, but I thought it was an improvement.

I put up a pretty good front in public, but at home I became withdrawn and irritable. I had temper tantrums, and I spent a lot of time in my room, brooding under the covers. I hated it, but the *toogee* began to take over my life. When Mom questioned me, I clammed up. Mom and Dad should never, never find out about my life as a street kid. I was convinced that if they did, they'd shun me.

One night after Mom confronted me about my sullenness, I ran to my room, so upset that I didn't dare speak to her for fear I'd lash out and ruin everything. I looked in the mirror behind the closed door of my bedroom. "You haven't changed anything," I hissed at myself. "You're still nothing but a dirty *toogee*, a piece of trash."

I ran to my bed and buried myself under the covers fully clothed. Now you've done it, I thought, cringing. Mom and Dad are probably wishing they'd taken that little boy.

My bedroom door opened, and my father called softly, "Stephanie."

I pulled the covers away from my face and looked at him. His face was grave. "Oh, no. He's going to tell me they want me to leave," I thought.

He sat in a chair by my bed and reached for my hand. "Your mother and I want you to know that we love you very much, but you seem to have a hard time accepting that love. The time has come for us to release you to God. You know the Bible; I don't have to tell you that God loves you."

He fell silent, his jaw working as he groped for words. Finally he said, "Think of Jesus, Stephanie. He has walked in your shoes. He knows exactly how you feel. He's the only one who can help you." My father hugged me and left the room.

For a long time I lay there, turning over in my mind what Dad had said about Jesus. He was born in hard circumstances, straw was his blanket as it had been mine, and he had to flee because, like me, some people wanted to kill him.

For the first time in years I felt a strange sensation on my cheeks: tears. Deep inside me something hard and cold had broken—something that had been standing between me and the love of my dear family and God.

I wept for Jesus, who understood about love but had to die for us anyway. I wept for the girl who finally had been loved, but still had chosen to listen to the voices that taunted her. And I wept in relief; Jesus knew all about me and still loved me.

A sprout of self-worth started growing in me that afternoon. As my anger melted away, so did my sullenness and outbursts. I let my hair grow back naturally and threw away the blue contact lenses. And then one day I looked in the mirror, regarded the face smiling at me and said, "God thinks you're beautiful, Stephanie, and I do too."

Trains

Amber Scott

rains had always made me nervous. One foggy morning, patches of thick, gray fog hung over the countryside, and I might not have seen the flashing lights of the railroad crossing if I hadn't known the tracks were there. I'd driven that road hundreds of times on my way to classes at Ball State University. And every day I slowed down for those tracks, even though in three years I couldn't remember the last time I'd seen a train. Still, I was always careful. Trains make me nervous; they have ever since I was a small child. Those railroad cars are just too big and too noisy.

I don't like being first at a railroad crossing when a train is coming. This time, as I pulled up to the crossing, a freight train came into sight down the tracks. I'd have to sit in my car and wait—first in line—for the train to pass. It never occurred to me to try to beat it. As the train roared past, my car rattled and I fiddled around with a new CD I'd gotten over spring break the week before.

A flash in the rearview mirror caught my eye; I looked up and saw the glare of headlights piercing the fog. Out of nowhere, a red pickup truck broke through the haze and raced up behind me. He must be going sixty miles an hour, I thought. I watched for some sign that the driver was slowing down, but he kept barreling toward me. A single thought gripped me: he doesn't see me. I knew he would hit me. I gripped the wheel with both hands and braced my feet against the floorboards. I pushed my head back against the seat and closed my eyes. "Help me, Lord, help me." Tires screeched then metal smashed against metal. I screamed as my car flew forward with a violent jerk, and my head slammed against the windshield. Glass shattered around me, and the roar of the train filled my ears.

I don't know how long I sat there with my eyes shut.When I opened them, I realized that my ordeal had not ended. I was being dragged by the train. The impact had jammed my hood halfway under one of the cars, and the train was pulling me along with it. A scream caught in my throat. I tried to sit up, but my hair was caught in the shards of glass from the broken windshield. I grabbed at clumps of hair with my hands and tugged myself free. "This can't be happening," I whispered.

The passenger's side of the windshield was shattered; only a section in front of me was intact. The back of the car was crunched toward the front seat; the roof had caved down just behind my head in the driver's seat. But the train sound was deafening, plus there was the *clunk, clunk, clunk* of my car pounding against gravel and brush as the train dragged me farther and farther down the track.

But I was still alive. I almost couldn't believe it. I looked down at my hands. I had blood on my fingers and palms, and I could feel blood in my hair and face. If I hadn't died yet, I wasn't going to now. I was sure of it. But I knew I had to get out of the car somehow. I tried to think, but the noise made it hard to focus.

I was wedged in the middle of the train, too far back for the engineer to see me, especially in this fog. I looked out the window and watched my car bounce hard against the rubble below. I knew I couldn't jump out because the train was going too fast. I'd never survive the fall.

Then I remembered my cell phone. I grabbed it and dialed the number that came naturally: home. Mom didn't leave for work until 7:30, so there was still time. I held my breath. I couldn't even hear it ring, the roar of the train was so loud. Then I heard a voice, but it didn't sound like Mom. "You've reached 754 . . . The answering machine! "No," I screamed as I turned off the phone. I tried to remain calm. "She's home. She has to be home." I took a deep breath. The car was getting bounced around even harder now. I could feel it scraping the ground underneath me as I sat crouched near the floorboards. I had to stay calm. "Help me, Lord. Watch over me, Lord," I prayed, over and over.

I turned on the phone and dialed again. This time, I heard a faint voice break through the roar of the freight train. It was Mom! "Mom, Mom, I've been hit!" I could hear her say something, but the noise of the train made it hard for me to understand her. I was just about to tell her what happened when the line went dead. Deep down, I knew Mom couldn't help me now. I needed to use what little power I had left in the phone to call for help.

I dialed the numbers with a steady hand: 9-1-1. I heard some-one pick up. The voice on the other end was little more than a squeak. It sounded like a man, asking me a question, but I couldn't understand what he was saying. "Please, Lord, help him hear me," I prayed. "I can hardly hear you!" I screamed. "I need help!"

"Where are you?" The voice was still nearly drowned out by the train's roar, but I could hear the question this time. "Car!" I yelled back, not sure how to describe where I was, how many miles I'd traveled since I'd been hit. It must have been four or five minutes. It seemed like an eternity.

"Where are you?" he asked again. Maybe he couldn't hear me.

"Somebody hit me and I'm being dragged along by a train!" My voice broke and I choked back tears. "I'm so scared!"

"Are you in a car?" These were the last words I heard him say before the line went dead. The battery was dead. There'd be no more phone calls for help. The only one who could get me through this now was the one I'd been praying to all the way down the track: God.

I sat back in my seat, shut my eyes, and prayed over and over again, "Watch over me, Lord, watch over me, Lord." A sense of peace came over me for the first time in my horrible journey. "Watch over me, Lord." I knew that somehow, I would survive. I didn't know whether someone would see me and call for help or whether my car would break away from the train. But I was certain that God would protect me.

A loud *thud* and my eyes opened wide. The back of my car had caught on the pole of a railroad sign at a crossing, and it was now pulling me away from the train. With a violent jolt, the car landed upright on gravel, slid a little, then stopped near the tracks. I looked around and realized it was over. I was safe.

I don't remember getting out of the car, but I do remember staring in amazement at the wreckage. I don't think I realized just how bad the damage was until I stood back from the car and took it all in. The front of the car, the roof, the back seat had all been crushed around me. Pieces of metal and glass were all over the place, but that small area where I sat, crouched down in prayer, remained untouched. A protective dome had formed around me, and shielded me from harm.

"Thank you, Lord!" I cried. I'd prayed to God all the way down those noisy tracks. And he'd heard and answered.

Trapped Underwater!

Sunshine Rolle

I headed out to my high school's parking lot, still humming a song from *Bye Bye Birdie*, which I'd just been rehearsing in the auditorium. Cold drops of rain splashed onto my head and arms that November evening as I tried to find my parents' minivan in the foggy darkness. Keys in hand, I unlocked the door and tossed in my backpack before settling into the driver's seat. As I checked the rearview mirror, I caught a glimpse of my gold angel necklace glinting in the streetlight.

"When I can't watch over you, I want God's angels to," Mom had said when she clasped it around my neck. My mom worried too much about my five brothers and sisters and me. Being the baby of the family, I got the brunt of it, especially now that my older siblings had all moved out. Mom's concern felt like a heavy cloak on my shoulders that I could never shake off. Like when she'd left for Nebraska a few days earlier to visit my sister and her newborn son. My dad didn't go, but he worked long hours as a university professor.

"Are you sure you'll be okay?" Mom asked.

"Mom," I groaned, "I'll be fine. I can take care of myself."

"Well, just be careful, Sunny," she said, "and remember, if you need help, turn to God."

I wouldn't need help, though. After all, I was already a junior in high school and I'd had my driver's license for almost a year. I was busy with college prep courses, the volleyball team, and musical rehearsals, but I had no trouble handling it all.

I thought I'd take the shortcut along the river. Although I'd never driven it by myself, I thought it would be safer than the crowded highway. Squinting through the billowing fog, I tried to make out signs and landmarks. I pulled onto my route and swiftly shifted my gaze from the front to the sides to the speedometer, like when I'd been learning to drive. Settle down, Sunny, I chided myself, you've driven through much worse. This is just a little rain and fog.

I stopped humming so I could concentrate on the road. Thick white swirls hung above the trees. The rain grew louder; hail smacked the windshield. Even with the wipers on high, I could barely see. Now I wished I hadn't avoided the cars on the highway. I wanted the comfort of other headlights, some company in this murky mess. I clenched the steering wheel with both hands. Just ahead I could make out a sharp curve. Before I could brake, the van skidded downhill.

The van flipped over, hit the ground upside down, then rolled again. As water crept up my ankles, I knew I was in the river.

"Help me!" I screamed, even though no one was around.

I tried to open the door. It wouldn't budge. Now the water was up to my knees. Images of times with my family flashed through my mind: sunny-day picnics, holiday dinners, late-night talks.

I kicked again and again at the door. The water was up to my neck. Looking down, I saw my angel necklace floating on the surface. All at once, my mom's words came back to me: "If you need help, turn to God." I let my body go limp and closed my eyes.

"God, please help me," I called out. The water was still rising, now lapping at my ears, but now I was calm and confident. Some-how, some way I would get out of the van.

I struggled with the door again and cried out another prayer.

Time was almost up, but I wasn't afraid anymore. Underwater I groped for an opening in the van, a place where I could squeeze out. Suddenly I was in the river, gasping for air. My shoes and coat were as heavy as lead. "I have to keep moving," I told myself as I stroked and kicked through the water.

I pulled myself up onto a muddy shore and turned back to the sinking van; its windshield wipers were still whisking back and forth.

Ahead I saw an orange glow through the fog. I focused on it and tried to run, but I felt as though I were still moving through water. At last I saw the house with the light. I pounded on the door. A middle-aged woman opened it.

"My car," I gasped. "The water." She hastily took me inside and toweled me off, then called my family.

At the hospital, doctors examined me and found I had no broken bones. My back was sore and I had some bruises on my ankles, but that was it. Mom said that's all that was important.

The police asked me to help them locate the van. I showed them the curve where I'd gone off the road. Fifty feet down the embankment was the mud-covered roof of the van. The rest of it was completely submerged. After they dragged the van out, the police tried repeatedly to open the doors. They couldn't. They were jammed shut. The windows, too, were all stuck closed.

"I don't know how you got out of there," an officer said to me. It was a mystery to everyone, a mystery I couldn't begin to explain.

I walked up to the van and saw my reflection in one of the side mirrors. Again, my eyes were drawn to my angel necklace. I knew how I had made it out of the wrecked van. God watched out for me, ready to help me even though I thought I didn't need him.

Of course, Mom still worries. But now her worry feels more like a cozy blanket than a heavy cloak. Every day I wear the angel necklace she gave me to remind me of her loving concern, and of how God sent me an angel one rainy night to open the door to the rest of my life.

Volcano

Doug Nuenke

We stood at the summit of Mount Marapi, a volcano on the island of Sumatra in Indonesia. From the rim of the crater, my friends John and Kristi and I stared in to the gaping volcano. It looked harmless enough, an ashen depression half a mile wide with a still pond in the middle. At one end steam hissed from the hidden fissures, and I could hear what sounded like bubbling lava.

"I can't feel any rumbling beneath my feet," John joked.

"Not today," Bruce said. "Last time I was up here, we couldn't get this close. The volcano was blowing ash and steam."

Bruce, an American, was our guide. He taught English in the nearby town of Padang. John, Kristi, and I were part of a group from the University of Kansas that was spending the summer studying Indonesian culture. A hike up the volcano seemed a welcome break from our all-day language classes.

In the predawn darkness, we had struggled up the steep narrow trail. The sky was filled with stars, and every once in a while we spotted the flashlights of other hikers. The morning air was crisp and clear; rain clouds that usually shrouded the peak hadn't rolled in yet. In fact, getting lost in a fog bank seemed to be our greatest danger. Even so, we had prayed that God would guide and protect us on our hike.

"We should head back now," Bruce said.

We stepped carefully around deep cracks reeking of hot, sulfurous air. The rim of the crater was lined with charcoal-gray lava and ash. Nothing grew here, no ferns, no grass. It seemed as barren as the moon.

At nine we took a few last pictures of the view, then turned down toward the tree line to the start of the trail. Thirty yards from the rim the earth suddenly shook. There was a frightful rumbling, then the volcano erupted, and an enormous red-hot fountain of rock and ash spewed from the crater.

We raced down the plateau leading to the trailhead. The exploding lava rock sounded like a gigantic waterfall, and the air was filled with hot ash. Pebbles and boulders showered down on us. I put my backpack over my head seconds before a rock hit my back and knocked me flat. Then a softball-size missile struck me. When I struggled to my feet, I was lost in a dense cloud of swirling, hot, black sand. I smelled the pungent odor of burning hair and felt my head. It was wet and sticky with my blood. With my head bleeding, my clothes full of holes where the pellets had burned through to my skin, and my back throbbing, I was the only person around.

Then, suddenly, the volcanic cloud lifted and my friends emerged, ash-covered and supporting one another. As the volcano rumbled again, we rushed behind a large stone and huddled together.

The eruption stopped, but we knew that it could start again. Kristi's entire right side was scorched where her windbreaker had burst into flames. John's left arm was swollen and he was limping badly. Bruce had ugly burns on his back and a huge gash in his calf.

"Will anybody come to rescue us?" I asked Bruce.

He shook his head. "Not a chance. Nobody will want to face the poisonous gases, lava, suffocating ash. We're on our own."

Limping and bleeding, we stumbled onward, searching for the

trail. Kristi was the one who could walk best, so she went on ahead.

When we had started our hike that morning, we had marked the trailhead by wrapping toilet paper around a nearby tree. We wondered if it would still be there. Kristi found the trail, and we limped forward. Every step I took was painful, and John could barely walk.

We decided that Bruce and Kristi, who were the most mobile, would move as quickly as possible in hopes of getting help.

The steep trail was littered with roots and fallen trees. Every step was painful for John. After twenty minutes, he had to rest. "I need to sleep," he begged. "Let's stop here."

"No," I said. "We've got to keep going. The volcano could erupt again at any moment."

When John's eyes began to roll back in his head, I shook him, "You can't sleep; we've got to move on."

By mid-afternoon, it began to rain, and the trail quickly became a slope of slippery mud. John fell a dozen times, and he was coughing up blood.

"Not much longer," I told him.

We had been hiking for six hours and there was still no end in sight. Then I spotted a fallen tree that I recalled from our hike up. "John," I said, "remember the tree? I think there's just a half hour to go." Minutes later I caught a glimpse of the valley below. I had misjudged the distance. We still had several hours of hiking ahead of us. We would never make it.

"God," I prayed desperately, "you have to help us down this mountain. We can't do it on our own."

And there, in the dripping rain, I knew that God had already given us the strength to get this far. He was still with us, and we could go on.

"Come on, buddy," I said to John. "We can make it."

The evening light was waning when we finally neared where we had parked our Jeep. Suddenly I heard the sound of rushing water;

and the seven-foot-high banks of the stream ahead had turned into mud slides because of the rain.

As I stood there wondering how I could get John over the water, four Indonesian hikers joined me on the bank. "We'll help," one of them said. Quickly and carefully, he and his friends lowered John down the slope, carried him across the stream, then lifted him up to the other side. We quickened our pace as we walked to the car. When we reached the Jeep, Bruce and Kristi were waiting, exhausted. We climbed in and Bruce drove us to the hospital. It had been nearly nine hours since the eruption.

At midnight, Bruce and I were released after having our wounds stitched and our burns treated. John and Kristi spent the night in the hospital, and the following day they were flown to Singapore for additional care.

When I awoke in the morning, my body was covered with burns and large bruises. My windbreaker, shirt, pants, and shoes were filled with holes where rocks had burned through. My canvas backpack contained volcanic rocks that had seared through the fabric. Everything inside was ruined, including two metal film canisters that had been crushed to half their width.

Only then did I grasp how close we had been to death. God had protected us when the earth moved and the mountain rumbled. And I knew he would be with me whenever I needed him.

One Deadly Drive
Wally Crowder

I sat in the driver's seat of the big, shiny black Lincoln Continental and stared past the end of the pier in San Pedro, California. For a moment I felt butterflies in my stomach again. At the last minute you always feel a little bit of hesitation, a temptation not to go through with it. But I knew I would. In minutes I would be driving that Lincoln at full speed straight off the end of the pier and into the Pacific Ocean. I didn't intend to die or be injured. I'd planned this very carefully, I thought. I'm a stuntman. That day I was working on a TV movie and doubling as a gangster who, literally, takes a long drive off a short pier.

Although I thought that I had planned for every eventuality in this stunt, I knew there was always a small chance of an accident. That's why I had been extra careful and hired a "safety," another stuntman who would ride with me as a passenger. If something went wrong, one of us could help the other. I never could have foreseen that I'd need much more than just a safety on that stunt.

I had been in the stunt business only a couple of years when I accepted this job, but by now I was experienced enough not to be worried. I had raced stock cars for years, and the transition to full-time stunt work was not much of a leap. I was moonlighting as a driver in auto commercials when I was asked to do my first stunt. The director decided he wanted to use two cars in the commercial instead of one. He planned a stunt in which the two vehicles would race toward each other and, after hitting a mark, stop on a dime, and wind up nose to nose. The driving coordinator asked if I thought I could do that. Piece of cake. The driving coordinator was impressed, and so my career as a stuntman began.

A stuntman is not a daredevil who spent his childhood picking fights and falling out of trees. He's more of an athlete, a professional whose motto is always "safety first." That is why we had taken every precaution that day in Los Angeles Harbor. And, because we only had one car, we would use multiple cameras but only do one take. It had to be perfect the first time.

While I sat in the car and waited for the cameras to roll, I went over my safety checklist. This pier was fifteen to twenty feet above the water, higher than is safe. The car should land flat on the water—more time to get out before the car sinks. The longer the drop from the pier, the more time for the heavier front end of the car to hit first and drag you down. Cars float for vastly different periods of time, depending on their make and construction.

The Lincoln was much heavier than most cars. Ideally I wanted to be out of the car before it sank. Safety divers had already gone down to check how deep the water was and what was on the ocean floor. They found the water dark and murky, and the bottom covered with silt and mud. With any luck, I'd never see that.

I had reinforced the car's windshield with heavy Lexan, an industrial-strength plastic. Normal windshields are made of safety glass; with an impact at forty miles per hour, they're gone. I had added a metal roll bar across the inside top of the car to keep the roof from caving in, in case the car flipped over and landed upside down. We left the electrically powered windows open. Inside the car, we'd installed five-point seatbelts, the kind race car drivers wear. The belts go over the shoulders, across the waist, and between the legs. An Aqua-Lung was bolted next to me in the car, with an extra tank of air that would be enough for one hour underwater. Besides the usual film crew, two safety divers were underneath the pier in case of an emergency, for example, if I lost consciousness.

On this day, my biggest decision had been to hire a safety to ride in the car with me. For the camera crew this would be a "long shot," filmed from a distance. Since the audience wouldn't be able to see who was in the car, I could have belted a mannequin to the passenger's seat to double for the second gangster; but the drop was so long and a Lincoln is so heavy that I decided it was worth it to split my earnings with a safety.

The cameras started to roll. The director gave us the signal. I stepped on the gas. The pier blurred past us as we picked up speed. Then we were airborne, flying between sky and sea on a breezy California afternoon. Immediately the front end dipped down. We hit the water at an angle, and the impact was intense. The windshield exploded, and shards of glass tore my face. Saltwater rushed in through the jagged, gaping hole in the windshield. The force of the water pinned me back, and within moments we were swallowed up by the muddy water.

I fumbled for the catch that would release my seatbelt. Across the seat from me, the safety, not confined behind a steering wheel, was able to move much more freely. He unbuckled his seatbelt and struggled out the side window. I last saw him swimming for the surface.

I began to panic. The car was flipping over and I couldn't tell which way was up. I knew I should stay in the car until I hit bottom and I could get oriented. I went down very rapidly. I grabbed for the Aqua Lung. The car landed upside down and then sank into four feet of mire and slime. I was buried upside down in mud forty feet underwater. Mud clogged my eyes and nose. I couldn't see. I couldn't free myself from the seatbelt. Visibility was zero. It could take the divers hours to find me. Blood was rushing to my head. I could lose consciousness. The pro who was trained never to be stuck without a way of escape was helpless.

I was panicking, telling myself that I didn't want to die, when out of nowhere, in a clear voice, came the order, "Relax, stupid." Two words spoken in a calm, friendly, commanding voice. Who spoke them? Could it be God? But does God call people stupid? Yet the intimacy of the words, the good-natured jibe, almost made me laugh. That was exactly what was needed to cut through my terror. "Thanks Lord," I said in my mind.

He was right. I had been stupid. There was no reason to panic. I had air. I was conscious. I had everything I needed to get out of the situation.

I relaxed. The mire eventually settled. Slowly, gingerly, I found the twisted buckle to my seatbelt. I undid it. While still upside down, I located the crushed roof and felt around for the open rear window. I wiggled out of it and swam to the surface.

Air has never tasted sweeter than it did that day off the San Pedro pier. I didn't even notice that my face was streaming with blood until I was safely on land.

I have learned a number of things because of the incident. I learned that when driving a car into water, I must add a second duplicate windshield on top of the first with chicken wire in between. I learned to take down a pink balloon that I could let out of the sunken car to bring the divers straight over to me. And I developed a way to foam the trunk and the back seat so that even if a heavy car goes under, it will bob back up.

But the most important lesson I learned in a stunt, as well as in the tough situations of life, is don't panic. That's what the voice was telling me under forty feet of water. Be quiet. Think things through. It's in the quiet that we can find a way out.

Lord, when my soul is weary
and my heart is tired and sore,
and I have that failing feeling
that I can't take any more;
then let me know the freshening
found in simple, childlike prayer,
when the kneeling soul knows surely
that a listening Lord is there.

RUTH BELL GRAHAM

Faith That
Loves

Pickle

Gina R. Dalfonzo

Dear Mrs. Pickern,

It's been over seven years since I left your fourth grade class and over six years since I last saw you. But your influence has stayed with me, and it always will. You see, God put you into my life just when I most needed you, and used you to teach me a lesson I'll never forget.

I was almost nine years old when I first met you. I came to Immanuel Lutheran School, adjusting from a move and shell-shocked from a year of public school. To call me shy and reserved would have been a gross understatement. Yet you, also new to Immanuel that year, captured my interest from the very first. I had never had a teacher like you before!

One of my earliest memories of you is that green dress of yours. Remember? You told us that you loved green and that you had a special green dress you liked to wear. Because of that dress (and your last name), some of your former students had started calling you Pickle. From that moment on, you were either "Pickle" or "Mrs. Pickle" to all of us.

Most of my memories of you are of the funny things you did. You could always make us laugh; you were forever saying or doing something crazy. Sometimes we felt as though, on the inside, you were no older than we were—but not just because of your silliness. It was also because you understood us so well.

There was that matter of the plastic bags, for instance. Most of us had some in our lunches, and we delighted in blowing up and popping every one we could lay our hands on. After several attempts to put a stop to the incessant noise, you finally came up with a solution. Every Friday, if we had kept our bags quiet for the rest of the week, we would have a "Pop Day." Everyone would save his bags from lunch, and on the count of three we would all destroy them at once.

The idea worked perfectly. As lunch drew to a close each Friday, students scrambled to collect every bag in the vicinity. We would then all blow up our bags and join you in the countdown. Then—*bang*! An explosion almost lifted the roof off the building. That had to be the best method of discipline ever used.

Of course, your ways of controlling us weren't always that enjoyable. Do you remember how, whenever we were noisy, you would write the letters of the word quiet on the board, one at a time? Most days we only got as far as U or I. But if we ever reached the T, some form of mass punishment would result. I can still remember myself and a few others, when you had left the room for a moment, jumping up from our seats in panic and calling, Shhh! She's coming! We're gonna get a T!"

So while we considered you our friend, we also maintained a healthy respect for you—and not just because of the Q-U-I-E-T. In fact, looking back on those days, what most impresses me is how you managed to be a wife, mother of two, teacher of two grades, girls' soccer coach, and pianist for our school choir. You always kept such a cheerful attitude through it all. Somehow you found the time to let each of us know that we were special to you. And now that I'm in high school staggering under my own workload, I've started to wonder how you handled all of that.

I think the answer can be found in my favorite and most vivid memory of you. With your love and encouragement, I had come a long way that year. I had begun to come out of my shell and make friends. I was even starting to develop a (slightly nutty) sense of humor. Deep down inside, though, I was still the same shy, sensitive little person I had always been.

On this particular day, several of us were passing out papers that you had graded. Returning to my seat, I suddenly stopped short, staring down at my desk in horror. There lay an assignment that I had done several days ago. Glaring up at me was a big red F!

It couldn't be. There must be some mistake! I had never received an F in my life; in fact, my grades were usually among the best in the class. But there it was—I had failed. I sank into my seat, red with shame, and quickly stuffed the offending paper into my desk. As I looked up, I saw you watching me silently, and I hastily dropped my gaze. How could you do this to me? I wondered unhappily, though I knew that you hadn't really had anything to do with it. Fortunately recess came a few minutes later. I wandered out and stood by myself in the school yard, watching my classmates on the playground. I was trying as hard as I could not to cry, when you came out and put your arm around me.

I don't remember word for word what you said to me that day, but your message comes back to me very clearly. You explained to me gently that one F wasn't the end of the world, and that I mustn't take every failure to heart. As I remember that conversation, it seems to me that you understood me almost better than I understood myself.

My problem wasn't that I was afraid to fail; it was more that I didn't know how to fail. Up to that point I had been successful in almost everything I did: report cards, piano lessons, ballet classes. You wisely saw that as I got older, I would inevitably fail again, and at more important things than a fourth-grade homework assignment. You must have known that if I didn't learn to deal with failure then, I might end up with a real problem someday.

I heard someone say once that we need to stop taking ourselves seriously and start taking God seriously. That pretty well sums up what you told me. When we learn to get our eyes off ourselves and look at him, we develop a confidence that nothing can take away. This confidence lets us laugh at ourselves and, more importantly, get up and go on instead of dwelling on mistakes. That, I believe, was how you could handle so much so well.

I've had to remind myself of that often, and maybe I'll always have to. But with the help of the Lord and my memories of you, I'm learning to trust him with everything—even the occasional bad grade! Your words and your example taught me one of the most important lessons I'll ever learn. Thanks, Mrs. Pickle.

Love, Gina

Father's Fishing Rod

Joshua Klein

t so happens that my father likes to tell stories, often of no particular relevance except for the fact that he likes them. While I grew up under this sort of tutelage, it took me until I was into early manhood to recognize the value of this ritual.

Besides being a would-be storyteller, he is also a fisherman of sorts, inasmuch as he loves to fish. There was one story that he used to tell every time he went fishing, often with me sitting blackly in the car beside him, having been threatened (I felt) into going on another fishing expedition. The story would occur when we were packing up the car, on the way to the fishing site and while we unloaded the car. He would tell it again as we rowed the boat out to the middle of the lake, and as we fled knots and untangled lines. That story was the tale of my father's fishing rod.

When my father became a young man, his father took him to the local store and, with great care and much father—and—son love, bought him a fishing rod. I could never tell what was so special about the rod, but my father always handled it as though it were either very expensive or highly explosive. He would relate to me over and over again, each time his eyes misting over and his face beaming in a sort of private joy, how he had caught his first fish with it. And if I did not change the subject soon, he would go on to relate the tale of each and every fish he had caught with it thereafter. But it was made clear to me at a young age that when I was old enough I could use the rod, and as it was rather outdated and my father had other rods better suited to his advanced frame, I ended up using it most of the time.

Like most teenagers, I was usually difficult to deal with. My parents have loved me, and always will love me, truly and with all their hearts. But I think it was around the age of thirteen that I really tested the lengths to which they would go to continue loving me rather than simply breaking my neck. That year we went on a family vacation around the San Juan Islands, traveling in a boat my father had rented. It was incredibly beautiful country, and even my teenage bitterness and cynicism faded after a few late evening sunsets and early-morning sunrises. I had even managed to get on fairly well with the family, and had stormed out of the cabin and onto the boat top only a few times the whole trip.

Near the end of the trip I was allowed to sleep up top. That meant an evening of relative privacy for me, a precious commodity. It also meant being able to fall asleep with the stars as my roof and the gentle sounds of the ocean as my lullaby. Not that I would have admitted it then, but the idea rather appealed to me. I even submitted graciously to the idea of fishing for a spell before turning in, laying the rod beside me as I read a favorite book by lantern light.

The moment was a perfect instant in all things: the sunset's last glimmers just disappearing on the horizon, the stars coming out in the velvet sky above. And on a little boat was a little boy, just getting up to unroll his sleeping bag and go to sleep . . .

And then it happened: *Plunk*. Just a gentle plopping sound as the world around me began to spin and I turned to see my father's fishing rod, his pride and joy, sink beneath the inky waves.

There were frantic moments of running about, splashing with the net and the eventual discovery of what happened. Then came the anguished cries of my father. Huddled in the bow, amid the extra life-jackets and ropes and other sundries, I cried and cried. I prayed for the first time since I had been allowed to skip church, and I prayed for everything from forgiveness to death.

The whole time I was concerned most not by fear of my father or punishment, but by the dreadful fact that I had hurt my dad. In those few short minutes, I realized that I loved my dad. And that no matter what, no matter what happened, I always would.

There was no way to pay back what that rod represented. I could never take him back to the days when his father was alive and escort them to the town store. All those boring times I had listened half-heartedly to the story about the fishing rod suddenly seemed immeasurably precious, moments to be treasured for all time.

Eventually my mother asked me to come out, and the family spoke for a long while. We spoke of grief, and my father told me that he didn't hate me for what had happened and that it was okay. He told me that he still loved me and that he always would. And we cried together as a whole family—me, my sister, my mom and my dad. And eventually we all went to bed and fell into a deep, sad sleep.

The next morning my father and I got up quietly and went to pull up the crab pots. We smiled a little at each other and didn't say anything, because we didn't have to. The sun was high and the waves were blue, and even though something horrible had happened it was okay, because we both loved each other and that was enough.

As I set a crab pot down with a *thunk* on my side of the boat, I turned to hear a gentle laugh coming out of my father. His crab pot was beside him on the deck, and he was leaning over the edge of the boat, carefully pulling on something. A fishing line was tangled in the crab pot, and he was slowly trying to retrieve whatever was at the other end.

Then in the quiet morning air, my father and I gently pulled his fishing rod up from the bottom of the ocean and cried and laughed together until my mother and sister woke up to join us.